Engaging the Resistant Child Through Computers:

A Manual to Facilitate Social and Emotional Learning

By Maurice J. Elias, Ph.D.,

Brian S. Friedlander, Ph.D.,

and Steven E. Tobias, Psy.D.

DUDE
PUBLISHING

**A Division of
National Professional Resources, Inc.
Port Chester, New York**

Publisher's Cataloging-in-Publication
(Provided by Quality Books, Inc.)

Elias, Maurice J.
    Engaging the resistant child through computers : a
manual to facilitate social & emotional learning /
Maurice Elias, Brian S. Friedlander, Steven E. Tobias.
-- 1st ed.
    p. cm.
    ISBN: 1-887943-51-X

    1. Handicapped children--Education--Data processing.
2. Computer-assisted instruction. 3. Affective
education--Data processing.   I. Friedlander, Brian S.
II. Tobias, Steven E. III. Title.

LC4024.E45 2001   371.9'04334
                          QBI01-201089

Cover design by Faith E. Deegan
Book design by Liz Kingslien, Lizart, Tucson, AZ
Pagesetting by The Service Bureau, Alice Bowman, Tucson, AZ

©2001 By Maurice J. Elias, Ph.D., Brian S. Friedlander, Ph.D.,
and Steven E. Tobias, Psy.D.

Dude Publishing
A division of National Professional Resources, Inc.
25 South Regent Street
Port Chester, New York 10573
Toll free: (800) 453–7461
Phone: (914) 937–8879

Visit the NPR Web Site: www.nprinc.com
Author's Web Site: www.eqparenting.com

Printed in the United States of America

ISBN 1-887943-51-X

Dedication

To my occasionally resistant but always wonderful children, Sara Elizabeth and Samara Alexandra.   (MJE)

To my wonderful wife, Helene, who gives me the support and encouragement to follow my dreams and to my wonderful daughter, Chelsea, who brings joy to our world.   (BSF)

I dedicate this book to my children, Meg and Gillian. It is for them that I work and for them that I try to improve the world.   (SET)

▶ Also By The Authors

Emotionally Intelligent Parenting: How to Raise a Self-Disciplined,
Responsible, Socially-Skilled Child

Raising Emotionally Intelligent Teenagers:
Parenting with Love, Laughter and Limits

By Maurice J. Elias, Ph.D., and Steven E. Tobias, Psy.D.

Social Problem-Solving: Interventions in the Schools

Problem-Solving/Decision-Making for Social and
Academic Success

By Maurice J. Elias, Ph.D.

Social Decision-Making and Life Skills Development:
Guidelines for Middle School Educators

Coauthored By Maurice J. Elias, Ph.D.

Promoting Social and Emotional Learning:
Guidelines for Educators

Group Interventions for the Promotion of Social Competence

Building Social Problem-Solving Skills:
Guidelines from a School-Based Program

Social Decision-Making Skills:
A Curriculum Guide for the Elementary Grades

Teach Your Child Decision-Making

▶ Contents

▶ *Acknowledgments*

Professionals from many fields have shared a great deal of their time and expertise with us to enable us to produce this book. In the area of assistive technology, we would like to thank Tom Caine, from Tom Caine & Associates for his support and for providing many of the hardware and software tools for individuals with special needs which are referred to in this book. Likewise, we would like to thank Robin Duncan of Knowledge Adventure for providing us with the latest version of Hyperstudio. We would like to thank Lester Ray, of Apple Computer for his support and his vision of how computers can impact on the lives of the students we work with. Lastly, we would also like to thank Mike Thorpe of Acrux Software who has given us the opportunity to work with his wonderful multimedia application *İBuild* .

Among clinicians, we have benefited from the ideas and input of Dr. Steven Gordon, who helped field test some of the techniques mentioned in the book. In the schools, we give special thanks to Vicki Poedubick, who has piloted our earliest techniques and continues to work with us on expanding the use of computers and technology in the area of social emotional learning. We wish to give special thanks to our families, who understood the importance of this project and gave us the time we needed to complete it, and to Michael Kline and Trina Epstein, who worked with many of the techniques in this book and provided much of the material in chapters 3 and 4, respectively. Finally, gratitude is expressed to Robert and Helene Hanson and their team at National Professional Resources who believed in this project, worked on it with great care and creativity, gave it a marvelous visual look and feel, and continue to believe in the importance of our approaches. This book would not have come into existence in this form without National Professional Resources' vision and help.

This section introduces and provides a rationale for using computer software in clinical practice with children from preschool and elementary age through adolescence. We first present a brief review of the literature, then discuss the usefulness of computers as a clinical tool to quicken engagement and establish a therapeutic relationship. Computers are both familiar and inviting to children, making their use a natural means of enhancing the therapeutic process. In this managed care age of short-term therapy and documentation, the computer can make the therapeutic process more efficient. In addition, most clinicians have computers in their offices but have limited understanding of their broad usefulness. With this book, we hope to encourage clinicians to do as we and other colleagues have done—use accessible computer technology to create cutting-edge therapeutic techniques and improve engagement with children in counseling.

We emphasize that the computer is a tool to enhance therapy, not supplant the therapist or the vital relationship between therapist and client. Each chapter will highlight a traditional clinical activity, such as exploration of feelings or problem solving, discuss the use of commercially available software to enhance this activity, and walk the reader through step-by-step examples. In addition, each chapter presents a focal case as a model.

Many of today's children, including very bright ones, have difficulty sitting, communicating, and expressing ideas to others. This situation makes traditional ways of counseling and psychotherapy with children—talking therapies—very difficult. Even play therapy does not appear to engage children as it once did, and certainly it is not for students as they move closer to junior high/middle school age.

As clinicians, we are now working with the MTV/Microsoft/Mac/Pentium/PlayStation Generation. Technology serves as a bridge to engage these children. The resistance that we used to encounter becomes replaced by openness. What used to be a major struggle now goes more smoothly and often is, dare we say it, more fun.

Of course, the computer does not replace a clinician, school psychologist, counselor, social worker, or other trained professional. Rather, it is used to enhance the therapeutic relationship and to help the child or adolescent achieve a greater degree of interpersonal interaction with the therapist and adult. Think of it as a tool for the clinician to engage in the play therapy of the 21st Century!

Television, video games, and computers have become caretakers, mentors, and playmates to many children. In this age of short-term therapy and counseling, the computer can be a quick rapport builder. But it is more than that. It is an exemplar of working through what Howard Gardner has called the multiple intelligences, using a combination of motion, sound, color, text, and physical activity. It engages spatial skills, cognitive skills, and, as we will show, emotions. The computer becomes a tool for positive self-exploration and change because it allows children and adolescents to work in a context of strength as opposed to a context of deficit.

▶ Why Does This Work?

Foremost, the computer is nonjudgmental. Errors can be made, but the computer does not criticize. Further, errors are more easily fixed on a computer than they are in real life. A drawing can be changed and a word corrected later, so that the flow of thoughts and feelings can occur with less interruption and censorship. Especially for children who are socially withdrawn, rejected, or hostile, the fact that they are interacting initially with a machine reduces the threat to them. Children who avoid contact with clinicians will gaze at a computer screen.

▶ How Computer Techniques Complement Child Treatment

Child treatment is simultaneously simple and complex. Changing behavior is always a difficult task. When parents and other caregivers bring their young children, in whom they have invested so many of their hopes and dreams, to be "changed," they are entrusting the clinician with an awesome responsibility. Yet, there is simplicity to the therapeutic process. For more than any specific thing a therapist says or does, there is one fundamental precept that must be followed: Caring relationships provide the foundation for all learning, including the learning that is involved in therapy and counseling (*Lessons for Life*, 1999).

Recent work in the area of emotional intelligence (Cohen, 1999; Elias, Tobias, & Friedlander, 1999) has led to a renewed appreciation of the role of affect in therapeutic gains. Human memory is encoded in terms of information, context, and affect. This has important implications for what children take with them when they leave counseling sessions. Clinicians have long experienced, and discussed, disappointing generalization from therapy. Emotional intelligence theory suggests that the context of therapy is important for learning to be transferred into everyday memory, cognition, affect, and behavior. Generalization of learning, including therapeutic skill development and insights, is fostered when learning takes place in situations that are not highly noxious, in which there is hope and expectation that the learning can be put to use, and the individuals in the learning situation feel both self-efficacy and support for carrying out what they have learned (Salovey & Sluyter, 1998).

Clinicians must provide an environment in which children feel psychologically safe, are willing to share their thoughts and feelings, and believe that what is happening is relevant to them and their lives today. The use of the computer facilitates these dimensions. Computers in counseling confer instant relevance. We don't have to just sit and talk. Certainly, there has been a considerable increase in the use of therapeutic games. But kids' own game playing has shifted more to video-computer modalities. Clinician and child share a feeling of safety when they focus on the computer, rather than on the child's problems. Opportunities to work with the computer on neutral tasks and hear the therapist's approval and praise make the child more willing to share. Paralleling this process, activities within each chapter of this book follow the progression of beginning with the hypothetical, moving gradually toward the personal, and then reaching the more emotionally charged (Elias & Tobias, 1996).

Larry Cuban, writing in *Education Week* (Cuban, 1999), estimates that 7 in 10 teachers now use computers in their homes, and this number is rising. Fewer teachers use computers in their classrooms, however. This paradox reflects how benefits of technology are not going to be maximized in educational settings for the foreseeable future. Children who need, and can benefit, from technology-based solutions to behavioral and academic problems will tend to get services from school psychologists and technologically oriented private practitioners. And there is mounting evidence that computer-assisted treatment has distinct advantages to traditional talking therapies.

Recent research has examined the role of written expression as a means of emotionally processing difficult experiences. Among the mechanisms that appear to be operating is that writing:

- **allows for venting of emotions**
- **gives individuals a chance to reappraise what took place**
- **promotes taking alternative perspectives on what happened**
- **provides verbal labels that allow events and feelings to be examined and understood more coherently than previously (Esterling, L'Abate, Murray, & Pennebaker, 1999).**

L'Abate (1999) has gone further and stated that the successful interventions of the future will involve writing outside the therapist's office. He believes that talk, as a primary medium of therapeutic change, has reached its peak. Interestingly, as children spend more time on email and instant messaging (IM'ing), they spend less time communicating via talk. L'Abate sees the computer as growing in importance because it extends important therapeutic processes efficiently and effectively beyond the actual session. Responding to criticism that data increasingly show the efficacy of psychotherapy (Cummings, 1999), L'Abate points out that while this may be true, the intrusions of managed care and other forms of time limitation, such as those found in many busy schools, create contexts in which data have not shown the effectiveness of psychotherapy. He reasons that computer-assisted interventions have the potential to reach many populations that could not be reached if talk and face-to-face contact are considered prerequisites for helping (L'Abate, 1999a, p.229).

Growing recognition of the shift in many children from auditory to visually centered learning also supports the use of computer-based approaches as an adjunct, or even full partner, with talking approaches. In schools, children at all grade levels encounter visual tools such as thinking maps, brainstorming webs, concept maps, and task-specific organizers. These tools serve to integrate:

- **auditory/written language and visual/pictorial images**
- **linear thinking and non-linear, holistic thinking**
- **isolated facts and bits of information and related concepts, patterns, and inter-connections**
- **what is known with what is not known, or received and constructed knowledge (Hyerle, 1996).**

Bringing this array of tools into therapeutic work is enhanced tremendously by the use of the computer and its ability to provide visual representations. Of course, auditory integration is provided through clinician-child dialogue, as well as auditory media brought into the computer. Overall, the computer modality provides for continuity with techniques that many clinicians consider staples in their therapeutic toolbox.

Relationship to Existing Therapy Techniques.

The use of the computer is consistent with, and in many ways serves to enhance, the efficacy of existing therapy techniques. Storytelling in its various forms is transformed into printed text that can be enriched via different fonts, pictures, clip art, and even sound. There are formats to allow the creation of short movies and multimedia slide shows. Many of Richard Gardner's (1976) approaches, such as mutual storytelling and the use of games, helped inspire the computer applications presented here. Various forms of drawing, the use of charts, social problem solving, cognitive-behavioral techniques of looking at consequences and formulating plans, and the use of role play all have been adapted for the computer.

In each instance, experienced clinicians, as well as trainees under supervision, have used these techniques. They have been used by those whose computer knowledge and comfort has been limited to their word processing software. As noted earlier, working with the computer helps to create a therapeutic climate and relationship. Especially for resistant children, the computer fosters a kind of mutuality that is not as apparent in more typical clinical encounters. Indeed, there are times when the child helps the clinician to get things set up, and this in itself helps build a positive mutual relationship, as long as the child's help is accepted gratefully, of course.

▶ *Who Can Use This Book?*

We are practicing clinicians and school psychologists, and we have written this book for school psychologists, social workers, guidance counselors, clinicians, and others who work with children in a therapeutic capacity. We recognize that these professionals will need ways to engage children who are hard to reach, reluctant to sit and talk, and used to the activity and pace of school life and their computer and media entertainment. This manual acts as a bridge between clinical needs and children's preferences for engaging activities. The activities have been used in private practice, schools, and psycho-educational clinics.

Minimal Computer Literacy and Hardware Required

Feasibility is what puts food on our families' tables. Minimal computer literacy is assumed on the part of both clinician and client. This book is based on knowledge of basic word processing or integrated application programs. The computers necessary are those which run these basic software programs. Specifically, those that use Macintosh computers of the PowerPC, iMac, G-3, or G-4 varieties will have no difficulty at all with the techniques presented here. Similarly, PC users with Pentium II, III, or Celeron processors will be able to perform the vast majority of activities, and those with MMX capability, which most PC's now have, can perform all of the multimedia applications.

Familiar Techniques Adapted to Computer Modality

Experienced clinicians will see familiar techniques adapted creatively to a new medium. In this book, we also show, step-by-step, how accessible computer technology can be used to create cutting edge therapeutic techniques. Readers will find these techniques compatible with various theoretical orientations.

Therapists who use projective instruments, play therapy, cognitive therapy, story telling, and ego psychology will find something familiar and of value to expand their repertoire, effectiveness, and efficiency. Clinicians who follow a variety of models from traditional independent private practice to problem-focused, short-term therapy will be able to use these techniques either as a primary form of intervention or as an adjunct.

▶ *Evidence of Effectiveness*

We are bolstered by knowing that the literature on the role of computers in treatment is small but solid. Computers in psychological treatment have been used in a variety of ways. They have been used for stress-related conditions (Colby, Gould, & Aronson, 1989), assertiveness training (Lieff, 1987) and in the development of interpersonal skills (Campbell, Lison, Borsook, Hoover, and Arnold, 1995). More generally, a study demonstrated that simply learning how to use standard computer software, such as word processors and painting programs, enhanced self-esteem and mastery in chronic psychiatric patients (Mahler & Meier, 1993). Another study using standard software demonstrated that these tools engaged children in treatment, and made possible the discussion of important issues during therapy (Kokish, 1994).

Computer games, such as role playing and fantasy games, have been used with some success in treatment situations (Favelle, 1994; Resnick & Sherer, 1994). In addition, successful experimentation has begun on the use of computer-based simulated environments in the treatment of acrophobia (Rothbaum, Hodges, Kooper, Opdyke, Williford, & North, 1995). Another simulation-based program has demonstrated the ability to enhance the moral development of youth in distress (Sherer, 1994). In fact, these simulation methods are proving so compelling that an annual conference is held at the University of California, San Diego, on the clinical applications of virtual reality.

Finally, data have demonstrated that people are more likely to share difficult, personal problems with a computer rather than with a stranger (Plutchick & Karasu, 1991). In our own work, we have found that computer technology has been an important clinical aid with our most troubled children, allowing for rapport building and skills building (Elias, Tobias, & Friedlander, 1994). Overall, what evidence exists for computer use in treatment has been quite favorable. But at least as important is that the computer-based activities were well received. Children enjoyed them and clinicians found them workable and efficient.

This manual is poised to be the first of what will become a standard type of clinical resource. It will serve as an engaging springboard for a new generation of clinical and psychoeducational procedures, friendly to the efficiencies of managed care and attuned to the seemingly ever-growing difficulty and elusiveness of clinical engagement of today's technologically and media sophisticated children and adolescents.

▶ *Format of the Book*

The chapters of the book have been selected and ordered to reflect basic elements of therapy and relatively simple applications of computer technology. We begin with establishing relationships, the cornerstone of any therapeutic work. Basic drawing and painting applications are used to help children identify different feelings and then gradually depict what they are feeling. The next element is sharing, because, without sharing, there is precious little for the clinician to do. It is especially important to help children share feelings related to significant emotional events. For years, clinicians have used stories as a way to accomplish this. For today's children, multimedia storytelling is something they are comfortable with and gravitate toward.

Lasting change is enhanced by self-reflection, and we link this to self-exploration via multimedia autobiography. Here, we encourage clinicians to begin in a context of strengths, as a way of getting to know a child, who she or he is, and what kinds of activities define his or her identity. As children become comfortable authoring a story about their lives, the potential increases for them to disclose the story of emotionally charged or otherwise difficult or troubling aspects of their life, past, present, and future.

Chapters 5 and 6 shift the focus slightly in that they address areas that many clinicians might want to get into quickly, depending on the child's approach to the treatment, and time parameters that unfortunately may be imposed by managed care, an overwhelming caseload, or other limiting circumstances. In Chapter 5, we tackle the issue of giving a child a sense of hope about him- or herself.

For too many children, even a positive therapeutic relationship and enjoyable experiences in treatment do not translate into significant changes or gains in their social world. Often, what must be changed are children's beliefs about themselves, their worth to others, their capabilities, and their potential. We sometimes have to unlock children's dreams about who they are and what they can become.

In our experience, using the computer to create personal print ads, commercials about oneself, and related self-promoting activities, accomplishes this important therapeutic task. Not only are the activities valuable, but printing out the products of these activities allows them to be shared with others who are valued in the child's life. In addition, these ads and commercials help bolster a child's confidence between sessions, serving as tangible reminders of the child's worth.

Chapter 6 brings a focus on skills children need for effective interpersonal relationships. A special program to create short movies is used to set up interpersonal situations to which children want to learn to better adapt. Children are then helped to construct scenarios for how to handle these situations effectively. In the process, they learn individual and group skills for approaching others, including how to approach others in a group, knowing what to say and how to say it, and how to be cooperative in a group. In this chapter especially, role play is used in conjunction with the computer to either pre-test what goes into the movie or to test out what is put in the movie before it is considered finalized.

Chapter 7 takes the work done in Chapter 5 to a more advanced level, both in terms of the therapeutic depth and the software required. In Chapter 5, the focus is on, "What's good about me?" and "Who am I and what do I want to become?" This chapter is more likely to be useful with teenagers, as it encourages them to look to the future and create alternative possibilities for various life tracks on which they might be headed. Although we discuss specialized software that is well suited for these therapeutic goals, it is possible to adapt the techniques to more commonly available software packages, as described in the chapter.

Chapter 8 is reserved for teaching a problem solving strategy. We use one based on extensive data and that is consonant with the principles of emotional intelligence (Elias & Tobias, 1996; Elias, Tobias, & Friedlander, 1999; Goleman, 1995). With regard to the latter, we refer most critically to the role of feelings in serving as a cue that there is a problem to be solved, and a guide to the framing of that problem. The overall approach is guided by the mnemonic, FIG TESPN, which stands for the following:

- **FEELINGS cue me to thoughtful action.**
- **I have a problem.**
- **GUIDE me to a goal.**
- **THINK of things I can do.**
- **ENVISION outcomes.**
- **SELECT my best solution.**
- **PLAN the procedure, anticipate pitfalls, practice, and pursue it.**
- **NOTICE what happened and now what?**

We present two software programs that have been tested, one primarily for elementary school children and the other for those of middle-school age and older, to build skills in everyday decision making and problem solving. Both programs provide written printouts to serve as aids beyond the therapy sessions. The Interactive Course in Social Problem Solving, based on the **iBuild** software program, begins by helping children with "readiness" skills in preparation for problem solving. For example, they learn how to keep calm so they can start thinking and problem solving, how to recognize their "feeling fingerprint" and feelings in others. The Personal Problem Solving Guide takes children through the problem solving steps, either in response to trouble they have gotten into that they would like to avoid in the future, or a problem they are anticipating and want to develop plans to address. Chapter 9 is devoted specifically to the use of the Personal Problem Solving Guide and related techniques. In our experience, problem solving is an essential skill, basic to much that occurs in counseling. Teaching this skill in a way that children will learn and generalize, however, is difficult. Therefore, we present this complex and integrative skill at the end of the book. We conclude the book with Chapter 10 and a discussion of adaptive technologies and a variety of ways to make accommodations for children with special learning needs.

▶ *A Word about Application of These Techniques in Schools and Homes*

We have tried to not always use clinical language. Why? Many of the techniques in this book are fully capable of being used by teachers, pupil services providers of various disciplines, and parents. While these are powerful applications in clinical and counseling contexts, there is much here of a broad practical use. So, we ask you to read this book creatively and look for ways to put these helpful ideas to work. Anyone who wants to reach out to reluctant youth will find that, for many of them, the computer can be a valuable ally.

Chapter Format

Chapters 2–9 follow a specific, common format:

- **Therapeutic Uses/Goal**
- **Overview of the Activity**
- **Time Frame for the Activity**
- **Clinical Rationale**
- **Developmental Considerations**
- **Minimum Materials and Optional Materials**
- **What to Prepare in Advance**
- **Conducting the Activity Step-by-Step**
- **Preparing the Child**
- **Doing the Activity**
- **Ending the Activity**
- **Clinical Case Illustration**

To orient the clinician to the goals of an activity, we begin by listing what specific problems or therapeutic tasks can be accomplished by its use. We continue with an overview, so the clinician can be clear about what it is that the child and therapist will be doing. An important aspect of this, of course, is the time frame. The Clinical Rationale is followed by Developmental Considerations, both of which help clinicians to make sure the activity being used is appropriate and, within that, that the approach taken is best matched with the clinical situation being faced. Throughout, we also indicate how the various techniques presented in the context of specific clinical examples also can be used with many other clinical situations.

To help get clinicians logistically ready for working with a child, we indicate the materials needed and other matters that might need to be prepared in advance, such as pictures, other personal items, or written work that a child might need to bring from home. The core of the chapter is, of course, step-by-step guidance for carrying out the activity. We have grouped this into three general areas: preparing the child (what to say, how to explain what will happen), performing the activity (the specific interaction around the computer, including detailed procedures for all aspects of the computer work), and ending the activity (how to bring it to a close psychologically and technologically, in terms of saving work done).

We conclude each chapter with an illustrative case presentation that shows how the computer-based activities have been used to engage children of various ages efficiently and provided both information for, and a bridge to, more traditional clinical methods.

In the following chapters, you will find detailed guidance to move your treatment into the information age and the age of technology. By so doing, you increase your ability to reach and connect with children for whom talking therapy feels like an unnatural or threatening situation. Hit the power button, load your software, and get ready to enhance your vision of child treatment!

References

Campbell, J., Lison, C., Borsook, T., Hoover, J., Arnold, P. (1995). Using Computer and Video Technologies to Develop Interpersonal Skills. *Computers in Human Behavior*, 11(2), 223–239.

Cohen, J. (Ed). (1999). *Educating Hearts and Minds: Social Emotional Learning and the Passage into Adolescence*. NY: Teachers College Press.

Colby, K.M., Gould, R.L., Aronson, G. (1989). Some Pros and Cons of Computer-Assisted Psychotherapy. *Journal of Nervous and Mental Disease*, 177(2), 105–108.

Cuban, L. (1999). The Technology Puzzle: Why is Greater Access not Translating into Better Classroom Use? *Education Week*, 18(43), 68, 47.

Cummings, N. A. (1999). Comment on L'Abate: Psychotherapist Future Shock. *The Family Journal: Counseling and Therapy for Couples and Families*, 7(3), 221–223.

Elias, M.J., & Tobias, S., E. (1996). *Social Problem Solving Interventions in the Schools*. NY: Guilford.

Elias, M.J., Tobias, S.E., & Friedlander, B.S. (1994). Enhancing Skills for Everyday Problem Solving, Decision-Making, and Conflict Resolution in Special Needs Students with the Support of Computer-Based Technology. *Special Services in the Schools*, 8, 33–52.

Elias, M.J., Tobias, S.E., & Friedlander, B. S. (1999). *Emotionally Intelligent Parenting*. New York: Harmony/Random House.

Esterling, B., Abate, L., Murray, E., & Pennebaker, J. (1999). Empirical Foundations for Writing in Prevention and Psychotherapy: Mental and Physical Health Outcomes. *Clinical Psychology Review*, 19(1), 79–86.

Favelle, G.K. (1994). Therapeutic Applications of Commercially Available Computer Software. *Computers in Human Services*, 11(1/2), 151–158.

Hyerle, D. (1996). *Visual Tools for Constructing Knowledge*. Alexandria, VA: ASCD.

Kokish, R. (1994). Experiences Using a PC in Play Therapy with Children. *Computers in Human Services*, 11(1/2).

L'Abate, L. (1999). Taking the Bull by the Horns: Beyond Talk in Psychological Interventions. *The Family Journal: Counseling and Therapy for Couples and Families*, 7(3), 206–220.

L'Abate, L. (1999a). Decisions We (Mental Health Professionals) Need to Make (Whether We Like Them or Not). *The Family Journal: Counseling and Therapy for Couples and Families*, 7(3), 227–230.

Mahler, C.R. & Meier, S.T. (1993). The Microcomputer as a Psychotherapeutic Aid. *Computers in Human Services*, 10(1), 35–40.

Plutchick, R., & Karasu, T. (1991). Computers in Psychotherapy: An Overview. *Computers in Human Behavior*, 7(1/2), 33–44.

Resnick, H., & Sherer, M. (1994). Computerized Games in the Human Services: An Introduction. *Computers in Human Services*, 11(1/2), 17–29.

Rothbaum, B., Hodges, L., Kooper, R., Opdyke, D., Williford, J., North, M. (1995). Effectiveness of Computer-Generated (Virtual Reality) Graded Exposure in the Treatment of Acrophobia. *American Journal of Psychiatry*, 152(4), 626–628.

Salovey, P., & Sluyter, D. (Eds.) (1998) *Emotional Development and Emotional Intelligence*. NY: Basic Books.

Sherer, M. (1994). The Effect of Computerized Simulation Games on the Moral Development of Youth in Distress. *Computers in Human Services*, 11(1/2), 81–95.

Working with the Alphabet:

ADHD, LD, MR, ODD, PDD

WORKING WITH THE ALPHABET

GOAL

"To reach the unreachable star."
Don Quixote from *Man of LaMancha*

▶ *Overview*

Highly verbal, cooperative children with good emotional control and long attention spans probably do not need therapy. At least we have never seen a child that fits this description in a professional capacity. The children we work with in schools, agencies, and practices are the ones who are not engaged with others and not easily engageable. Most have the diagnoses noted above: attention-deficit/hyperactivity disorder, learning disability, mental retardation, oppositional defiant disorder, pervasive developmental disorder, or some other psychiatric diagnosis such as anxiety or depression. These are the ones who are both hardest to reach and most needy. It is for these children that this book was written.

This chapter will highlight aspects of each of these disorders and discuss special therapeutic considerations when using computer activities with these children. It is not our intent to define each disorder or review treatment approaches. We are giving only a brief introduction with some ideas on treatment goals and how to work with each population. We encourage you to use your clinical insight and creativity to take the activities presented later in this book and apply them to the individuals that you work with.

▶ *Attention-Deficit/Hyperactivity Disorder (ADHD)*

ADHD is perhaps THE diagnosis of the late twentieth century. It seems like every child and his or her uncle was being referred and placed on medication. This disorder is characterized by deficiencies in regulation of impulse control, attention, and activity level. Often deficits in handwriting and social skills accompany this disorder. We will not get into the intricacies and controversies of diagnosis here. Suffice to say, one must see this disorder as a matter of degree, not of kind. But, in terms of treatment, we like to say, "If it is a problem for somebody, then it is a problem that must be addressed."

The computer seems to have been made by and for individuals with ADHD. It can bypass their handwriting deficiencies, provide them with the stimulation they crave, feed their need for immediate gratification, help them socialize at a safe emotional distance, and give feedback in a non-critical way. It makes the computer an enticing therapeutic tool to use with children with ADHD. This is not all to the good, however.

When working with ADHD children, it is important to maintain the social relationship. ADHD children can over-focus on the computer and try to use it in a way that excludes the clinician and the therapeutic process. We do not recommend using game playing on the computer as a rapport-building experience. The rapport that is built will be between the child and computer and not child and clinician. Games can be used as reinforcement for a productive therapeutic session.

For programs that require extensive typing, the clinician may wish to input information for the child, but the child will want to be very actively involved. Allowing him or her to control the mouse is usually a must. This can allow both of you to work together on a particular program.

Programs and activities that ADHD children can benefit from are ones that facilitate social awareness and self-esteem. If the child is on a behavior monitoring system, this data can be inputted to a spreadsheet and the progress represented by graphs and charts. The Hollywood High program can also help teach social cause-effect. With multi-media applications like Hyperstudio and PowerPoint, children can develop their own autobiography emphasizing their strengths, therefore building self-esteem.

▶ *Learning Disabilities (LD)*

LD is a very broad term that encompasses learning and processing deficits. Low self-esteem and behavior problems, especially in school, are often seen in children with learning difficulties. Again, we will not get into the issues of diagnosis, but prior to working with this population it is important that the clinician be aware of the child's deficits in order to accommodate for them. If there is an auditory processing problem, emphasis should be placed on visual stimuli. If there is a graphomotor deficit, an adaptive keyboard may need to be used (see Chapter 10 on adaptive technologies). Children with LD often have already experienced a great deal of frustration. In these activities, we are looking to bypass their source of frustration rather than remediate it.

It is also important that we identify and promote a child's strengths. It may be helpful to do a multiple intelligences assessment prior to working with the child. This will facilitate recognition of the child's areas of capability not only for working with the child but also for him or her to recognize and celebrate. The multi-sensory nature of computers is a primary benefit for this population. Any strength can be utilized. The computer can be auditory, visual, and tactile all at the same time. Use of multimedia, including graphics and music, are important to help students express themselves.

Clinicians may want to think about using programs such as Hyperstudio and PowerPoint with LD children. Also refer to the last chapter in the book to find out how you can use more specialized hardware and software to help LD children access the computer.

▶ Mental Retardation (MR)

The mentally retarded population is most difficult to provide therapeutic services to because of their relatively limited cognitive potential for self-awareness and insight. Therapeutic goals for this group, therefore, will be more limited. Children with mild to moderate levels of mental retardation (IQ 40 to 69) would potentially benefit, while, unfortunately, those below this level may not.

The most appropriate goals for this group in using the computer would be in the area of social skills. A deficiency in social skills is part of the adaptive skill deficit necessary to make the diagnosis of MR. The paradigm for teaching social skills to this population involves the sequence of teaching, modeling, and role-playing, and in-vivo practice with reinforcement. The computer can be helpful when teaching specific social skills such as feeling identification or problem solving. It is most important that generalization be facilitated. Once particular skills are taught via the computer, it is necessary to use guided practice with reinforcement out in the "real world."

Individuals with mental retardation will benefit from the auditory feedback that can be provided by using a talking word processor. Text that is typed into the word processor can be spoken by the computer. Activities that focus on social discourse and scripting of social situations are beneficial and can be teamed up with a talking word processor so that the individual can listen to it. Likewise, it may be necessary for the clinician to use an alternative keyboard (i.e., Intellikeys) so that it is easier for individuals with mental retardation to access the computer. Please refer to Chapter 10, where we discuss how to use alternative keyboards and talking word processors with pictures as an effective teaching tool with this population.

▶ *Oppositional Defiant Disorder*

Disobedience and acting out behavior are the most frequent reasons for referrals to therapists, probably because they are the hardest for others to cope with. These children are certainly a challenge to work with. Often they are dragged into a therapist's office quite unwillingly and do not wish to talk to a "shrink." By being in the therapist's office, the child perceives him- or herself as having a problem. Therefore, if he or she does not cooperate and gets thrown out, then he or she will not have a problem. These children also often have a negative self-concept and try to get others to reject them.

The computer is a welcome tool for anyone who has to work with this population. In addition to family and school-based treatments, it can also be helpful to work directly with the child. This is because few children are receptive to talking. Resistance is noted even with the therapeutic board games that are commercially available. Other board games or toys can seem too babyish. However, we have yet to see a child who does not want to play with the computer. One reason for this is that oppositional children are often not comfortable interacting with people and are more comfortable with machines. Initially, working with these children via the computer takes the focus off the interpersonal relationship with the child.

It may be necessary to first allow the child to play on the computer in the manner he wants in order to build trust and rapport. It is important to provide some games, which the child may enjoy, such as racing or adventure games. Try not to introduce anything too educational as they often have an aversion to learning. Use your clinical judgment (along with parental permission) regarding games with violence. It may sometimes be necessary to allow this type of play in order to engage the child at all. The goal is to ultimately move the child to more productive activities, using the games as reinforcement. We have found that this is also a good way to monitor progress. The more progress made therapeutically, the less interest the child has in violent games.

Almost any program that allows the child to interact and talk will be beneficial. This can be a drawing or painting program to express feelings, a program involving social situations that are created by the child, or role playing games where the therapist can discuss who the character is, how they feel, and why they behave the way they do. Programs that allow the child to create social situations and vicariously act out (Hollywood High, The Simpsons' Cartoon Studio) will yield fertile material for discussion.

▶ *The Autistic Spectrum Disorders*

These disorders include pervasive developmental disorder, autism, and Asperger Syndrome. The common characteristic of these disorders is the deficit in socialization. These children either show little interest in others or have a very limited repertoire of social skills and social problem solving behaviors. The development of language skills varies from well developed in Asperger Syndrome to sometimes nonverbal in autism. Cognitive skills tested in the mentally retarded range may or may not accompany these social and language deficits.

It is certainly easier to engage these children with the computer as opposed to a person, which makes the computer a perfect transition tool. A primary focus of treatment is often the teaching of appropriate social behavior. If positive social behaviors can be taught that are incompatible with inappropriate behaviors (self-injury, aggression, tantrums, etc.) then often the inappropriate behaviors will diminish. A standard treatment for reinforcement of target behavior includes praise and material rewards. However, use of the computer itself is often sufficient to ensure a child's cooperation within the session. When planning for generalization, the use of specific and relevant reinforcement in the child's environment will be necessary.

Skills important to address with autistic children are reading feelings in others and social comprehension. Children can be taught to focus in on specific non-verbal cues such as facial expression, body language, and tone of voice. Social vignettes can also be used to facilitate understanding of complex social interactions. Even short video clips, such as movie trailers taken off the Internet, can be used as stimuli for social learning. Clinicians should also use imitation and role-playing of stimuli presented on the computer to facilitate generalization. Having children participate in "chat rooms" with close monitoring can teach reciprocal communication.

▶ *Depression and Anxiety*

There is some controversy about what distinguishes a "disorder" from "normal" childhood depression and/or anxiety. This is especially difficult, as children do not manifest the same symptoms as adults. Often, some types of problems such as separation anxiety and conduct disorder are manifestations of an underlying mood disorder.

The computer is useful for dynamic assessment of emotional issues. Drawing programs and creative writing activities help the clinician assess and target emotional issues. The computer may also allow the child to express and explore their fears and anxieties at a safe distance. For example, one child who had a phobia of bees used the Internet to research bees. This indirect exposure helped to desensitize her.

In addition, both the child's cognitions and coping skills need to be addressed. Depression is associated with distorted cognitions about oneself, the world, and the future. Feelings of helplessness are also noted. The computer activities involving exploration of the self, such as creating an autobiography, can help children focus on their strengths and correct some of these cognitive distortions and negative self-images.

Teaching problem solving skills is also necessary to support children's coping skills and help them reduce some of the real-life stresses they face. The Personal Problem Solving Guide is one program that both addresses interpersonal problems and decision making as well as reinforcing a problem solving process.

The following chapters will review specific types of computer programs followed by examples of clinical applications. We have not attempted to provide you with a step-by-step treatment protocol for each disorder you may encounter. Rather, we have tried to give an overview of computer oriented techniques to add to your clinical tool chest. We urge you to be imaginative in using the computer with your clients. Sometimes the children will know more than you will and their ideas and interests can be usurped for more positive ends. Have fun!

Emotional Expression through Drawing/Painting

DRAWING/PAINTING

> ### GOAL
>
> *To foster emotional expression through
> drawing and painting programs.*

▶ Overview

This chapter will explain the basics of drawing and painting on the computer. The focus will be on the creation of a feelings library, a catalog of the child's visual portraits of various emotions with the potential addition of text describing experiences with these feelings. Items from the library can be inserted into any of the other documents a child creates using the techniques in this book. The feelings library can be opened at any time during the therapeutic process for reflections, modifications, or additions.

▶ Time Frame for the Activity

Clinicians should plan on working on this activity over a minimum two- to three-session time frame. Session one should be used to introduce the concepts and help children become accustomed to using the computer tools for drawing. Sessions two and three can then be used to allow children to explore their feelings by drawing them on the computer.

▶ Clinical Rationale

The therapeutic use of artistic forms of expression with children is not a new concept. However, the computer, acting as both easel and palette to the child, opens new vistas of clinical activities. Few children, even those refusing to draw on paper due to fear of failure or disinterest, will decline the opportunity to watch the almost magical process of their pictures coming to life on the screen. With a fairly simple set of tools, children of all developmental ages and stages are given a forum for their creative expression. This is a useful way to use clinically relevant material, particularly for nonverbal youngsters.

▶ *Developmental Considerations*

Many young children love to draw as well as use computers even though they cannot yet read or write. Literacy skills are not essential for this activity since the therapist can type the child's spoken words. As such, the creation of a feelings library is amenable even to preschoolers. In fact, preschoolers are at an age where they can benefit from being helped to associate their feelings with the appropriate labels. Drawing on the computer provides a fun way for this association to be accomplished.

On the other end of the age continuum, there is nothing to stop adolescents from creatively exploring emotions. They may enjoy working more metaphorically, perhaps drawing abstract or representational drawings rather than facial expressions. They may even wish to scan photographs into the computer symbolizing various emotions. A creative therapist can work with the youngster to develop the appropriate parameters for a given developmental stage.

MINIMUM MATERIALS	OPTIONAL MATERIALS	THERAPEUTIC APPLICATIONS
AppleWorks	Color printer	Identifying feelings
ClarisWorks		Self-understanding/
Kid Pix Studio		self-portrait
Corel Draw		Peer difficulties
Microsoft Office		
Microsoft Word		

▶ *Preparing the Child*

You may want to preface the creation of your feelings library by talking, and getting a sense of the child's knowledge of a range of feelings. It may be important to talk with a child about feelings, what they are, and what they mean. Role-play about feelings might also be used. Young children, or those who appear to have trouble expanding beyond happy, sad, and mad, may be assisted by being shown illustrations of facial expressions in books or even waiting room magazines. A mirror may be used so that a child may see what his/her facial features look like when pretending to feel a certain way. Sometimes it is useful to introduce crayons before using the computer. This can help set the stage for drawing on the computer. The advantage of using the computer is the ability to expand on the child's feelings vocabulary and store these words for future use. You may want to prepare by thinking about which feeling words to concentrate on, which may be a weakness for a child. Have some pictures of people's expressions available when working with the child to serve as a model. From our experience, children will find this activity to be motivating and will be increasingly inclined to discuss their feelings as they become more involved with the computer.

 **TECH TIP**

Just as libraries store books, some computer applications allow you the capability to store pictures in a library file, which can be quickly accessed. AppleWorks, which is available for Macintosh and Windows computers, will allow the creation of library files that can store individual sets of pictures that the children will draw on the computer. The Library Menu command is located under the File Menu. AppleWorks comes with preset libraries that will allow quick addition of pictures to your documents. However, the key to using libraries more effectively is to create your own so that the children you work with can store their feelings pictures easily and be able to reuse them.

 **THINGS TO THINK ABOUT**

If you have never used a program with a library feature, below is a quick tutorial:

❶ From the File Menu select Library.

Library ▶	New
Macros ▶	Open...
Mail Merge...	Animals
Page Setup...	Architecture and Design ▶
Print... ⌘P	Arrows
	AV and Technology Equipment
Quit ⌘Q	Awards
	Balloons
	Business Images
	Chemistry
	Common Symbols
	Community

2 Select New to create a new library file.

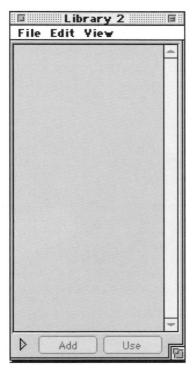

New Library

3 Draw a picture on the computer screen and select the appropriate selection tool.

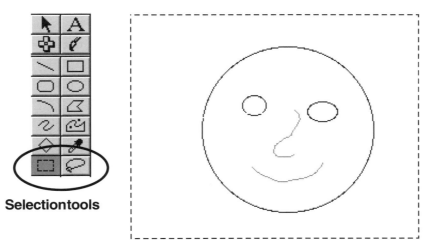

Selectiontools

Selection

❹ After you have selected the picture, click on the Add button on the Library window to add the picture. This will allow you to store the picture for future use.

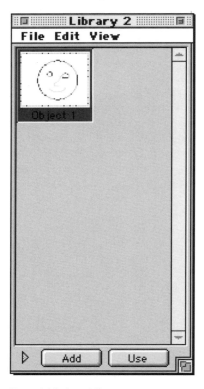

Face Added to Library

❺ Once you have added several pictures to the Library, go to the File Menu in the Library window and select Save. You can now save the Library files with a child's name and then retrieve it when you are working with the child during your sessions.

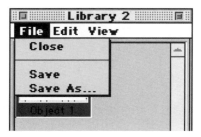

Saving a Library File

GETTING STARTED

The following example is based on using AppleWorks. Other paint programs have equivalent commands.

❶ Open AppleWorks and select Drawing under New Document.

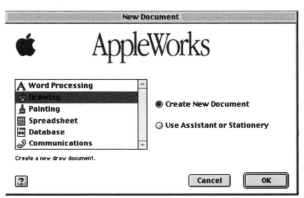

❷ It is a good idea to simply experiment with the drawing and painting tools in order to become familiar with them. Once it becomes comfortable, you can create a feelings library using the drawing tools or the painting tools.

The tools are as follows:

The meaning of *drawing* and *painting* with respect to the computer differs from our common understanding of those terms. *Drawing* on the computer refers to creating discrete shapes, such as lines or circles that can be selected, moved, or modified in certain specified ways, as well as deleted. What one draws on the computer can be thought of as an object with limited modifiability. *Painting* refers to freehand creation of shapes. To create a feelings library using only the drawing tools found on the drawing palette, tools such as the oval, the rounded rectangle, and the line can be used to create the head, eyes, and other facial features, as demonstrated below.

❸ Introduce the child to the painting and drawing tools and the palette of colors.

❹ Have the child draw a face on the screen (for young children, it may be easier to use the oval tool rather than paint freehand).

 **TECH TIP**

For children who are insecure about their ability to draw, it might be easier to begin by having them just click on shapes (the drawing tools).

Painting, on the other hand, produces images that are composed of pixels. Their modifiability is limitless, as illustrated in the examples below. Painting would be most appropriate if the client wished to create all the face shapes and features freehand.

❺ Discuss "how" this face "feels." If, for instance, the child says "happy," ask the child how he or she can tell that the face is "happy." Discuss the various facial features that fall under the rubric of "happy." As each feature is elaborated, ask the child to draw it on the face, or a new blank face. A discussion about the colors that are often associated with various feelings can occur at this point as well. If you have a color printer, add colors to the image and then see how they will look once printed out. You may want to ask the child to explain his/her choices as colors are selected.

❻ Now it is time to label the feeling. Click on the Text tool in the top right corner of the toolbox.

This changes the insertion point to the cursor used for writing. Have the child type "Happy." A young child can check spelling by utilizing the Edit Menu, selecting Writing Tools, and then selecting Check Document Spelling.

Happy

7 Ask children to tell you about one or more times, situations, contexts, etc., when they experienced the feeling they have drawn. For instance, the child can write about the sensory experiences that accompany each feeling, a time when he/she felt that way, or any other therapeutically relevant information. Remember, just click on the arrow in the top left of the toolbox and the insertion point will be changed to the cursor used for writing. Then, place the cursor where you would like your text to appear and encourage the child to begin to write about the context of the feeling.

8 Add the drawing to the Library by clicking on the Add button on the Library window. You can also copy the accompanying text into the Library with the picture by selecting both the picture and the text together.

Happy

I felt happy when my teacher said I did a good job on my homework.

When I'm happy, I feel warm.

9 At this point in the process, you might share an experience and ask the child to draw a picture that would accompany that specific experience. For example, you would say, "I just found out that a very close friend is ill. Now, draw a picture that would depict that feeling." Depending on the age and stage of the child, you may want to explore some of the following feelings:

*Happy	*Exhilarated
*Sad	*Bored
*Angry	*Disinterested
*Jealous	*Nervous
*Afraid	*Surprised
*Excited	*Confused
*Scared	*Irritated
*Dejected	*Overwhelmed

Because children view the world through their feeling filters, it is important to increase their feelings vocabulary and have them explore and talk about as many new feeling words as possible. You can explore when children noticed these types of strong feelings and how they handled it. The drawings are a wonderful way to link feelings with the child's personal experiences.

⑩ Place the face or faces in the child's feelings library that you created earlier in this exercise.

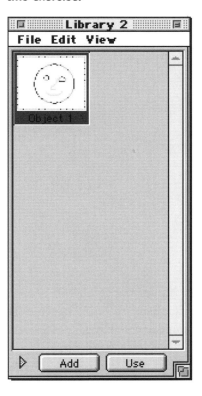

⑪ Save the Library file under the child's name for future use. Go to File Menu in the Library window and select Save As. Type "John's Feelings" (child's name) and click Save. Notice that the label of your library has now changed.

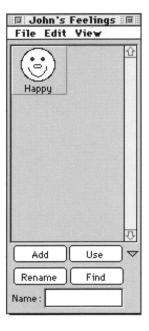

⑫ Print out a copy of the pictures in the Library file for the child. This library can now be opened at any time for the following purposes: to insert new feeling items, to pull items out for addition to a new document that a child is creating, or for future discussions, role plays, and/or other clinical activities.

◗ *Optional Techniques*

The activity described herein can be modified somewhat to create slightly different results. For instance, two separate libraries can be created and saved as "Feeling Faces Library" and "Feeling Words Library." A clinically relevant activity may consist of having the child match feeling faces with their labels. The Feeling Words Library can also be called upon when the child is having trouble labeling a personal feeling or when he/she is engaged in writing a story that requires the inclusion of feeling words.

◗ *Other Clinical Applications for Drawing/Painting*

A feelings library is just one way of making therapeutic use of drawing and painting on the computer. Many other libraries can be created, saved, called upon, and added to, around themes such as: favorite possessions, family members, friends, and favorite pastimes. The computer can be used for projective assessment via tests such as the "Draw-A-Person," "Kinetic Family Drawing," and the "House-Tree-Person." Of course, in such cases, the clinician would want to be sure to use the painting mode so that children would not be making their drawings with canned shapes.

The "Squiggle Technique," developed by noted child therapist Richard Gardner, wherein you would draw a squiggle for the child to develop into a drawing, is also a diagnostic and clinically relevant exercise that can be conducted in a fun way on the computer. You and the child can also take turns creating a drawing together, a technique known as "Mutual Drawing." Children can draw self-portraits, family portraits, favorite memories, and biggest fears. In sum, much clinically relevant material can be explored via computer technology in an engaging and non-threatening way.

CLINICAL CASE ILLUSTRATION

John was an eight-year-old child who was referred to the school psychologist by a teacher who was concerned about his social isolation and his guardedness in class. A consultation with John's parents revealed that they too shared these concerns. More specifically, they were worried about his anxiety level, his lack of friends, and his inability to "have fun."

When John was called in to meet with the school psychologist, his initial presentation was as a quiet and fairly withdrawn youngster. He was quite difficult to engage, making little eye contact and responding to questions with very few words. When asked if he could tell the psychologist about some of his "worries," he offered little.

In an effort to develop rapport with John and to ease him into the therapeutic process, he was asked if he liked using the computer. John made eye contact, smiled, and nodded yes. To start the activity, the psychologist drew a face and asked John to help her to identify what feeling the face represented. The therapist decided to draw several different faces with the following feelings: happiness, sadness, and anger. They talked about the feelings and wrote comments using the computer. This provided the springboard for John to begin to think about different feelings that he could express through his drawings. Then, it was John's turn. The psychologist and John spoke about some other feelings that he recently had, and then he proceeded to draw them using the computer. The psychologist and John spent some time talking about the feelings that he drew and then associating them with his own personal experiences. The psychologist explained to John that this was his feelings library and that it could be saved and used whenever he would like. Here is what John created during that first meeting with the school psychologist.

CLINICAL CASE ILLUSTRATION

JOHN'S FEELINGS LIBRARY

HAPPY

When I play with the other children at recess, I'm happy. This makes me want to go to school.

DISAPPOINTED

When I'm alone at recess, I'm disappointed. This means I need to go over to the other kids and ask to play.

WORRIED

I still worry sometimes, but I'm learning how to try not to worry about everything at the same time. Mom and Dad told me that that's a good start.

NERVOUS

When I'm nervous, I feel small. I'm learning to talk to myself when I'm nervous and how to take deep breaths to relax.

RELAXED

When I take my deep breaths that I've been practicing, I start to feel relaxed. I'm also learning to count to 10. This feels good.

PROUD

When I count to 10 and breathe good, I feel proud. I feel proud also when I go over to the other kids and ask to play with them. They say yes. I can do this! This makes me feel real big!!!

CLINICAL CASE ILLUSTRATION

John seemed to enjoy working on the computer and agreed to visit with the school psychologist again. They spent three sessions working on the feelings library together and talking about how we can help to shape and change our own feelings. The psychologist was now able to glean from this activity that the source of John's discontent was in part due to a lack of certain social skills and feelings of anxiety in social situations. By working on this activity, the psychologist was able to formulate a course of action, which would help John develop the social skills to make him feel more comfortable in the social arena. Additionally, the psychologist worked on some cognitive-behavioral strategies to help John feel more relaxed. By the fourth and final session, John left the school psychologist's office with a printout of the following feelings library, which he planned to share with his parents and his teacher (several contacts with both teacher and parents had been initiated by the school psychologist throughout the treatment). The therapeutic process and activities helped John discover strategies to deal with unpleasant feelings and introduced him to new feelings that previously played, at best, marginal roles in his repertoire.

CHAPTER

3

Exploring Significant Emotional Events through Multimedia Storytelling

MULTIMEDIA STORYTELLING

> ## GOAL
>
> *To foster emotional exploration/expression and perspective taking via the storytelling of important life events.*

▶ Overview

This chapter will explain the basics of how today's word processing programs can be used to help children unveil their innermost feelings about their life experiences. Children will be able to use text and combine it with pictures to put together a story, which can be thought of as a modern day projective task. When finished, children will have created a complete storybook (of one or more chapters) based on things drawn from their own lives. The story will consist of text, pictures/photos, and graphics on separate pages, much like any traditional storybook or computer-generated document. Youngsters with poor drawing skills have the benefit of cutting and pasting picture files as they explore their conflicts and problems in a creative manner. Using the computer, a child can edit the various elements of the story on the screen. Over the course of the time, the child will have the option of printing the story, and of making changes/additions as the treatment progresses.

▶ Time Frame for the Activity

The clinician should plan on working on this activity over a three- to four-session time frame. Plan during session one to introduce the concepts and help the child become acquainted with how to insert graphics and text into their word processing files. During session one, the clinician could begin to help the child think about what type of story he/she would want to work on. It is advantageous that some storyboarding is accomplished during the initial phase. This will help the child begin to focus and give the storytelling project a clear direction. The therapist may want to have some paper and pencils available to help rough out the story with the child. Sessions two through four can then be used to have the child develop the story on the computer. Throughout, the therapist needs to strike a balance between directing and allowing the child the freedom to express his/her other conflicts and concerns through the storytelling phase.

◗ Clinical Rationale

Children understand the basics of a story. A story has characters, a plot, a main idea, a journey and/or conflict, a beginning, and an ending. Stories have the potential to engage the writer on an emotional level, and also can provide the opportunity to gain a cognitive perspective on circumstances and important life events.

By having children tell a story from their own lives, along with your gentle exploration, painful and/or buried emotions can surface. The children can begin to place events in the context of the rest of their lives. A story is a wonderful metaphor for a child's life. Psychologists have learned that embedded into the stories of children and adolescents are conflicts, hopes, and aspirations, as well as problems that they face. Storytelling with the use of the computer adds another dimension. This is especially valuable for the child who may not have adequate verbal skills. As is often the case, many of the children and adolescents that are seen in counseling are not always verbal or communicative. This is one tool that is a real adjunct for these children.

◗ Developmental Considerations

With younger children, reading and writing ability must first be assessed before proceeding with the storybook. Young children might benefit from the use of a comic book format (perhaps even using familiar superheroes and plots). In addition, completing only one or two pages per session might be the maximum for younger children, whereas older clients might be able to, and be interested in, taking a chapter-per-session approach.

Having been exposed to more media in their lifetime, older children might want to include audio or video clips from television shows or movies that either have special significance for them or communicate something meaningful about their lives and experiences.

MINIMUM MATERIALS	OPTIONAL MATERIALS	THERAPEUTIC APPLICATIONS
Microsoft Office for Windows or Macintosh or comparable word processing program, Clip Art	Internet access, font library, audio (and/or video) clips, scanner, Sound Companion (sound editor), digital camera, microphone, color printer, a dedicated storytelling program such as Imagination Express: Destination Neighborhood, Storybook Weaver, Kidpix Studio.	bereavement, divorce, phobias, separation anxiety, understanding oneself, assessment of conflicts, sexual abuse, physical abuse, understanding emotions

▶ *Preparing the Child*

Consider prefacing the creation of the storybook with a discussion about story-telling (e.g., main components of a story, the child's favorite story or film and what they like about it, how it seems to work). Then, if the child is willing, try to together choose an appropriate topic from the child's life to write about. Preparing a formal list of information about the main characters and the story can be helpful as a guide for later development. If the child is resistant, a ficti-tious story or fictitious characters can be similarly employed. For many children, starting with a hypothetical is less threatening. You may at this point discuss the elements of a story, such as the setting, the characters, and their develop-ment. As noted earlier, this is a good time to talk about storyboarding. This helps to engage the child in the process and makes him/her think about the sto-ryline, setting, and the character development.

 THINGS TO THINK ABOUT

As you embark on this journey with a child, it is important for you to have at your disposal the necessary clip art that will then allow the child to develop a story line. Some of the children you work with may not have the graphic skills to draw free hand but can benefit from this activity with the use of commercially available clip art. Note that Microsoft Office comes with a vast array of built-in clip art.

Still, it may be helpful to have additional clip art files, which can be purchased inexpensively. Additionally, one can purchase sound clips, which can add a nice touch and keep the children you work with engaged in the activity.

GETTING STARTED

Prior to using Microsoft Word with the children you work with, it would be a good idea to set up the document and have the drawing tool bar accessible. From the File Menu select Page Setup and change the orientation of the page to landscape. Likewise, have your clip art CD-ROM available for use.

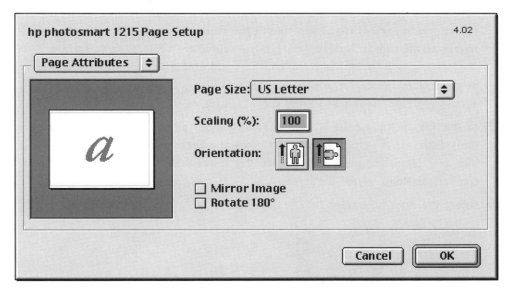

Landscape Orientation

❶ Open Microsoft Word and select New from the File Menu.

❷
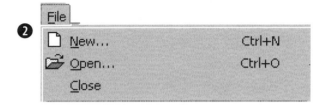

Introduce the child to the drawing tools and the clip art that are available for use.

❸ One of the key features of this activity is spending the time to help the child develop the story. Using a word processor, list the characters' age, interests, and something important that happened in the story. As you would with any projective or simulation technique, you can help guide the child towards certain themes and gain insight into the conflicts and problems that are present from how the child reacts. An initial story usually just gets the process in motion, with more "real" issues emerging subsequently.

❹ In this instance the child is writing a story about being in school and how he feels about it. The child decides to change the background to a light shade of blue and decides to use some clip art that is available in Microsoft Word. From the Format Menu, select Background.

❺ Select the light blue color for the background.

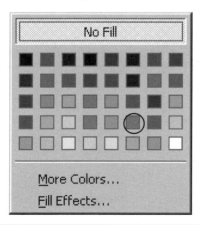

6 Now the child is ready to add some clip art and is looking for a picture of a student and a teacher. From the Insert Menu, select Picture, and then select Clip Art. Have the child peruse the clip art files to find the appropriate picture. While the child is working on the page in the story, you can be doing some facilitative questioning and ask the child to describe the characteristics of the teacher and the student in the picture. This will allow you to obtain some insight into what is troubling the child. Probes such as, "How do you think the students are feeling in the picture?" or "Tell me how you feel about the teacher," are diagnostically important.

❶ Blue background with picture of teacher with her students. Put some soft music in background.

Storyboard for First Scene

❼ The child begins to talk about the teacher's plan for Back to School Night and expresses to you that the students in the picture are feeling somewhat anxious about their parents meeting the teacher.

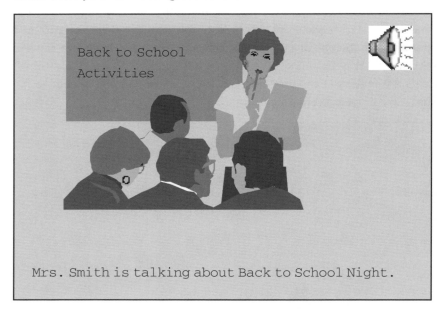

❽ Have the student use different fonts to highlight how he/she is feeling.

❾ Have the student add a sound file by Selecting Insert Movie from the Insert Menu. Sound adds a wonderful dimension to the storybook metaphor and allows the child to dramatize the mood through a sound clip. The graphic ◀️📢 in the story identifies the sound file. You and the child can just click on the triangle to hear the sounds and see what will work best.

 **TECH TIP**

Using a software program, like Sound Companion, with a microphone will allow students the opportunity to digitize their voice and include it in the story. Likewise, children can bring in their favorite music CDs and tape small snippets of their favorite songs to include in their story.

⑩ After the child has created the story, it is now time for you to print it for the child. You can now go back to the story and begin to tease out the underlying conflicts and help the child address fears, conflicts, and sources of anxiety. It is in the context of your relationship with the child that you can begin to more clearly identify the problem areas and chart a course of action. The storytelling activity opens the door and provides a bridge to the innermost feelings of the child. This activity has wide clinical application and is one that is easily managed within today's word processors. Having the ability to add text, sound, and graphics engages the child and frees him/her up to explore conflicts using a 21st century adaptation of the age old tool of storytelling.

Optional Techniques

Have the child print the story without page numbers (or even text) and ask him/her to rearrange the document to tell a different story.

Using Optional Materials

Internet Extra: Have the child search the Internet for clip art or video to download (landscapes, people, etc.) Suggested sites: www.altavista.com. Suggested search topics: clip art. Find free clip art at: www.clipart.com or www.pics4/learning.com.

Once the clip art is downloaded, simply select Picture (for clip art) or Movies (for video) from the Insert Menu.

Font Library: Have the child look through various text fonts and select an appropriate font (and size) for specific moments, feelings, or descriptions used in the story. For example, using a font named Tekton:

I was very scared of what was under my bed.

or, using Impact and increasing the size. . .

It was a very important moment in her life.

or, using a font named Zapf Chancery . . .

I had to be very careful of all the expensive, delicate things that my Mom had bought for the living room.

Microphone: Have the child provide extra detail in the story via the spoken word. This means that a small icon will appear in the document at a selected location, and the reader can click on it to hear a "secret message." To do this, pull down the Insert Menu and select Voice Annotation. Press the record button in the menu, and press OK when done. This will create a small icon, which can be placed anywhere in the document (via cut and paste) and played back simply by clicking on it once, and then double clicking.

Audio Clips: Have the child select music or sounds that tie into the story. These can be placed exactly where the child wants them in the story. The clip can be an important song, some background sounds (birds chirping, traffic noise, etc.), or appropriate catch phrases (from the Terminator audio clip library, "I'll be back," or from the Simpsons, "Don't have a cow, man.")

Scanner: Have the child scan in photos of important people/places involved in this experience. Simply scan in the photo/drawing using scanning software, and paste into the document where appropriate.

Scanned Image

Camera: Have the child take pictures of his/her face with different expressions to express the feelings at different points in the story. You can even use live-action video, if possible. Simply click on the Insert pull down menu, and select picture or movie.

CLINICAL CASE ILLUSTRATION

Sam was an 11-year-old boy who was brought to bereavement support services in a local hospital-based hospice. His mother was concerned about how he was handling his father's recent death. Sam's father suffered from a 3-year-long battle with lung cancer. Sam had been visiting his father in the hospital until the day of his death. Sam's dad had been a very outgoing and involved father. Over the course of his illness, he was progressively unable to attend important school events or family gatherings.

Sam presented as a very quiet, depressed young man. He spoke little during the first three sessions, and made very little eye contact with the clinician. Although his mother reported that Sam generally was talkative and enjoyed drawing, he showed no signs of engaging and refused to draw during session.

CLINICAL CASE ILLUSTRATION

At this point, the decision was made to use a computer-based approach. The clinician asked Sam if he enjoyed reading stories. Sam said that they used to have reading time in school when he was younger. From there, the discussion turned to different stories Sam knew, the stories told in television shows and movies, and Sam's ideas for what's important in a story.

The clinician felt that the most likely way for Sam to engage in the treatment was to encourage him to produce a multimedia story about a fictitious young boy's life. This was because Sam was far less likely to begin with a reality-based story, given that his father's death was still too emotionally charged and confusing to discuss directly within this new therapeutic relationship.

During this introductory session, Sam and the clinician decided on a main character, his age, his family, his interests, and something important that just happened in his life. All of these were put in list form on the word processor and printed out for Sam to take home.

Billy Myers
    10 years old
    Family: a younger sister (Janice), Mom, Dad, and a dog (Killer)
    Interests:

        drawing,
        baseball, soccer,
        Nintendo,
        going to friend's houses,
        eating pizza,
        family trips

    Event:

        who: Billy's Dad
        what: drove the car over Billy's bike and destroyed it
        when: last week
        where: in their driveway
        why: it was an accident
        how: he was late to work and didn't look in the mirror

CLINICAL CASE ILLUSTRATION

The clinician asked Sam to think about any other important information that should be included in the story, and to begin considering how the story should begin.

NOTE: Although the incident was based on something that actually happened in Sam's life several years before, the story was about a child's possession being taken away by a father who was very preoccupied and unable to attend to the personal property of others. This was a metaphor for Sam's relationship with his dad being destroyed by his father's death.

Sam began the next session excited about beginning the project, but the clinician took some time to discuss with Sam how the story should begin. They decided that giving some general background on Billy's family would be best.

```
There once was a family that
lived a happy life.  In the
family was a mom, a dad, a little
girl named Janice, a boy named
Billy, and a dog named Killer.
```

page one

CLINICAL CASE ILLUSTRATION

The clinician encouraged Sam to describe the father in as much detail as possible, such as describing what he looked like, and what kind of person he is.

```
The dad was an okay guy.  He worked very hard,
and didn't spend very much time with his
family.  He did a lot of things by himself.
Every Saturday he would leave early in the
morning, and go play golf.
```

page three

Because Sam was still becoming familiar with the equipment, this was the only page that was completed during this session.

In later sessions, Sam wrote about the bicycle incident, and the clinician paid special attention to exploring the reactions of the main character, Billy, to his father's carelessness.

Sam became more effectively engaged in the treatment as the clinician normalized the various reactions that a child would have to this incident.

CLINICAL CASE ILLUSTRATION

In subsequent sessions, the clinician encouraged Sam to write about how the main character was coping without his bicycle, and with his strong feelings towards his father.

```
Even though he didn't think it was the best
bicycle in the world, Billy used it a lot, and
it helped him get where he wanted to go.  He
wasn't sure if he would get a new bike.  He
was so angry at his father that sometimes he
didn't even feel like going outside to play.
```

page six

Finally, the clinician worked with Sam to explore, verbally and within the story, more about the father character. Had he always been inconsiderate? Did he want to destroy the bike and hurt Billy somehow in the process? What was his reaction to Billy's feelings about the broken bike?

After approximately 5–6 weeks in treatment, Sam began to speak of his father, and his father's death, in relation to the character of the father. Through this, the clinician was able to discuss more directly Sam's thoughts, feelings, and experiences surrounding his father's death. After a few more sessions, the therapy ended. The story was complete, and Sam received a color copy of his storybook to take home with him.

Self-Exploration through Multimedia Autobiography

MULTIMEDIA AUTOBIOGRAPHY

GOAL

To have students create a slide show that shares information about where they were born, their schooling, their family, and such things as interests and hobbies.

▶ Overview

In this exercise, the child creates an autobiographical slide show. The child or adolescent is encouraged to bring in pertinent information from home and school, which can be used to create the slide show. This activity is a wonderful icebreaker that can be also used to build rapport during the initial phase of psychotherapy. All too often, many children and adolescents who begin therapy are reluctant and resistant to share their personal history with the clinician. This is a particularly engaging activity for children that allows them the freedom to present themselves in a non-threatening manner. It is important to provide the youngsters with the framework for the activity and an opportunity to share something with you about themselves. This activity provides for rich diagnostic material as the youngster creates the autobiographical slide show. This activity may span several sessions. It is helpful to plan ahead so that the child can bring in pictures and personal items to enrich the activity. What is clinically interesting about this activity is that it helps the child engage the parents in discussions as to what to bring in, as well as where they can find out information about themselves that they may not know. Likewise, from a clinical standpoint, it is always interesting to consider what information the children are willing to share about themselves.

▶ Time Frame for the Activity

You should plan to perform this activity over a three- to four-session time frame. You should plan during session one to introduce the idea of an autobiography, and perhaps have on hand as a model some books of famous people who have written autobiographies.

❯ Clinical Rationale

An autobiography represents a comprehensive review of one's life. More than that, it is a time to step back, to reflect on what has been done, and where one's life is heading. This kind of self-exploration is easier for adults to do than for children or adolescents, but it is no less important. The multimedia autobiography is a means by which the clinician can engage children in an interactive activity that that will help them answer the questions, "Who am I?" and "Who do I want to become?" By encouraging children to create a slide show, it will help them to focus on their life and give you, the clinician, a jumping off point for discussion.

❯ Developmental Considerations

To a large extent, prior experience with computers may dictate what the child can do independently. Many youngsters in the age group of 8–10 are still not proficient at typing and may need to employ the use of the therapist for the typing of text. Also some of the students in this category may have perceptual-motor difficulties or learning disabilities, which may make it awkward to use the mouse or navigate through the files. Pre-adolescents and older children typically can engage in the basic activity and, if available, work with the options.

MINIMUM MATERIALS	OPTIONAL MATERIALS	THERAPEUTIC APPLICATIONS
AppleWorks or Microsoft PowerPoint	Scanner, digital camera, sound clips, and clip art	Identity issues, rapport building, peer conflicts, family conflicts, depression, school problems, physical abuse, sexual abuse, parent-child conflicts, and sibling rivalry

▶ *Preparing the Child*

Talk to the child about all the wonderful things that are usually included in an autobiography. Even resistant children are often excited about the prospect of documenting their life. Share with the child just how exciting it would be if he/she could develop an autobiography. Show samples of what a finished product would look like. Indicate that this one is special in that you will be using the computer to put together an autobiographical slide show. In session two and three, plan for the child to bring in pictures, family albums, birth records, and favorite music that can serve as the stimulus for both discussion and for entry into the autobiography.

 THINGS TO THINK ABOUT

It is important that the clinician be familiar with how PowerPoint operates. If you are not that comfortable with how it operates, feel free to use the built in Office Assistant to assist you as you are learning.

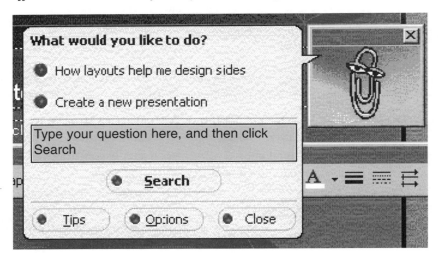

Office Assistant

Likewise, if you want to jump right in, select the AutoContent Wizard, which will take you step by step in helping to develop a framework for children to develop their autobiographical presentation.

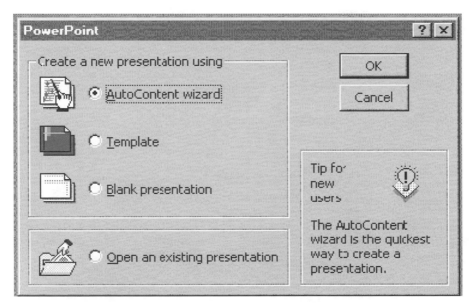

AutoContent Wizard

❶ Click the OK button to bring up the next screen.

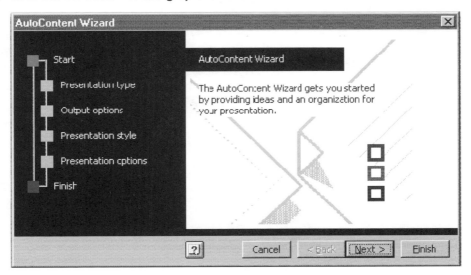

❷ Answer the prompts that appear, and click on the Next button. Before you know it, you will have created your first presentation slide. If your presentation opens up in the outline mode, go to the View Menu and select Slide.

❸ **View your first slide, which is the title slide.**

Title Slide

❹ **To create another slide, select New Slide from the Insert Menu. This brings up the New Slide dialog, which allows you to create different types of slides. Select the one with the black border around it and click OK. This type of slide will allow you to have both bulleted text and a picture on the slide.**

Insert Slide

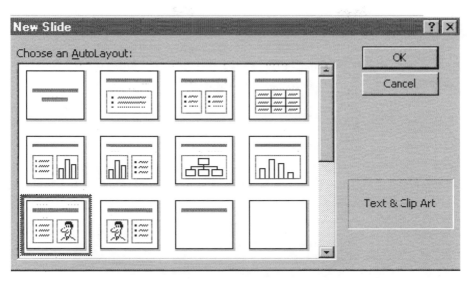

New Slide Dialog

❺ **In the first slide, the child may want to place a picture of when he/she was born and may want to add the hospital picture that is clip art. One can paste any picture onto the slide and then reposition by moving it. Here is an example of what the first slide might look like. Please note, the speaker icon signifies that a sound clip was inserted within the slide. You can insert sound clip files from the Insert Menu. Using the Insert command, you could then insert the sound files into the slide. There are many commercial companies that sell sound clips, or they can be downloaded from many of the online services or the Internet. It is a good idea to have some sound clips available to add to the slide presentation. Click on the sound to play it during the slide show. While working together, keep in mind that you are using the computer as a tool to engage and gain insight into the child you are working with. It is often helpful after the child has put together and constructed the slide presentation to ask him/her to narrate, and generally to explain his/her choices and thought process.**

6 To add text anywhere on the page, click on the Text box. Then, watch as your cursor changes to an "I" beam on the slide. Click and drag the cursor until you see a box. This is the box that you type text into. It can be repositioned anywhere on the screen by moving it with the mouse.

Text Box

Remember you can spell check all of your slides by going under the Tools Menu and selecting Spelling.

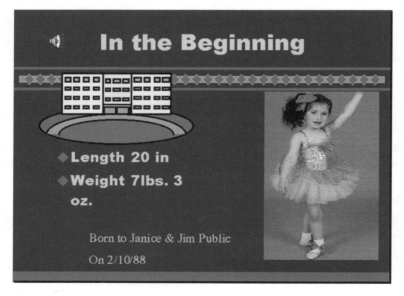

Slide One

7 Go to the Insert Menu and create Slide Two. After the child has had the opportunity to create several slides about his/her life, it is time to view the presentation. To view the multimedia presentation select Slide Show from the View Menu. Click your mouse on the screen to go from one slide to the next.

TECH TIP

Now that you have the basic idea of how to create a multi-media presentation, here are some tips that can increase the youngster's involvement even further.

- *Use the Quick Cam camera to create a small video that can be integrated into the multi-media autobiography.*

- *Have the child record small snippets of his/her favorite music that can be part of the multi-media autobiography.*

- *Have the child use sound clips to add special effects to the presentation.*

With a flat bed scanner, it is possible for the child to bring in some baby pictures and pictures of their family members that can be scanned and used as part of the slide presentation. Using a digital camera, it is also possible to take a current picture of the child and use it as part of the slide presentation by importing it into the slide presentation.

▶ *Clinical Application*

The above technique is applicable to many of the children and adolescents who are resistant to enter into a dialogue with the therapist. Using the slide presentation format with the computer engages them in a creative and non-threatening manner. It allows the child to select what parts of their life they are ready to share with you. Because the slide presentation can be saved to disk, it can always be considered a work in progress and revisited at various times throughout the therapeutic process. From a clinical perspective, the slide presentation can be considered and used in very much the same way a projective drawing might be analyzed. It is interesting to note what is shared and what a child omits. Key conflicts and stresses may be worked out through the presentation or denied. Keep in mind that you are using the computer as a tool to engage and gain insight into the children you are working with. It is often helpful after the slide presentation is constructed to ask children to narrate. In many respects, the computer becomes a key clinical tool in helping children communicate their inner lives without necessarily using verbal expression as the modality. This tool and technique also is ideal for youth you may see who have been sexually or physically traumatized and are initially unwilling to verbally express their feelings and thoughts with the therapist. However, they may be reluctant to work in chronological order because they are not ready to share aspects of their lives during periods of abuse. In these cases, just have them start with highlights of their choosing, and, gradually, as therapeutic rapport is built, work to fill in the gaps.

CLINICAL CASE ILLUSTRATION

Joan was a ten-year-old girl who was brought to the therapist's office at the end of September by her parents due to concerns and problems she was having with school refusal and separating from her parents. Joan was in the fifth grade and had just started a new school in the same district where she had been a student since kindergarten.

When the therapist initially met Joan, she walked with very little energy, behind her parents into the office. When she sat down, she made it a point to sit right next to her mother, as she snuggled up to her. She was rather reticent to talk to the therapist and had a difficult time maintaining appropriate eye contact. When the therapist would ask her a question, her mother would tend to answer for her. During the intake with the parents, the therapist could not isolate any known traumatic events or recent occurrences that could account for her sudden reluctance to go to school and her very clingy behavior, which started to become more noticeable during the two months prior to school beginning. While there were no significant changes in the family, Joan's mother had decided to return to work on a part-time basis once school began. With this as a backdrop, the therapist decided to use the Multimedia Autobiography activity over the next three sessions with Joan to learn more about her fears and conflicts, which may begin to explain her difficulties. After the intake, the therapist explained to Joan how the computer was to be used. This seemed to pique her curiosity. Joan and her parents were asked to bring in some pictures and information that she could use to create the Multimedia Autobiography activity during the next few visits.

CLINICAL CASE ILLUSTRATION

When the therapist met Joan for the second visit, she was more animated and eager to learn how they were going to use the computer during the session. The therapist explained to her what they were going to do and showed her a completed slide show. This slide show was put together by another youngster who had given permission for it to be shown out of his own enthusiasm for the approach and his wishes to help other children through this example. The therapist could immediately tell by Joan's body language that the Multimedia Autobiography had captured her imagination. She eagerly started developing her slide show. Joan was quite adept around the computer and fascinated with the ability to be able to scan images of herself at different phases in her life. The therapist noted, however, that Joan was rather a perfectionist and indecisive when it came to using different colors, frequently asking the therapist for an opinion.

Joan started her Multimedia Autobiography with a picture of herself that was taken shortly after she was born. She recorded the date of her birth and included a picture of her mother and father. She then created another slide of herself, when she was two years old, with her older brother, who was then ten, and her sister, who was fourteen. She seemed very content and happy while working on the slide presentation and spoke warmly and affectionately about her siblings. She then created another slide emphasizing her hobbies and interests. She included a picture of her flute and her dolls and made a comment to the therapist, "I really don't do this stuff anymore." The therapist asked her what she meant by the statement and Joan said, "For some reason I'm not interested in this stuff anymore." The therapist made a note of her response, and Joan continued to create the next slide, which revolved around school.

She used a piece of clip art of a teacher with several classmates involved in a math lesson. She portrayed herself as the youngster who was not paying much attention to the lesson and was reading a book. Joan went on to create a balloon and proceeded to type, "I wonder what Mom is doing now!"

CLINICAL CASE ILLUSTRATION

into the balloon. The therapist prompted her about what she typed and Joan explained that when she is at school all she can think about is where her mother is and what is she doing. Joan was visibly upset talking about what she had just said, and so, the therapist decided to wait until the next session to discuss the conflict she was having.

After each session, the therapist printed out a copy of the slides Joan had created and asked her to go home and reflect on them. Joan was a good writer and was comfortable writing down her thoughts and feelings about each slide. This proved to be a wonderful strategy, and when Joan came to subsequent sessions, she was more open and willing to talk about her feelings that were welled up inside her. This activity continued for a total of four sessions, after which time Joan became more comfortable with the therapist and could now more easily talk about her concerns and problems without the aid of the computer-based activity. The therapist learned a lot about Joan through autobiography, and subsequently learned that Joan was feeling rather depressed and had some strong attachment and dependency needs with her mother. The Multimedia Autobiography quickly allowed the therapist to engage the child in a strong therapeutic relationship and move into significant clinical issues.

Promoting Self-Esteem through Personal Print Ads or Commercials

PRINT ADS/COMMERCIALS

GOAL

*To have youngsters explore their roles and
perceptions of themselves.*

▶ Overview

In this exercise, the child creates a personal print ad or commercials for three
audiences—home, school, and friends. This activity allows youngsters to explore
feelings and perceptions about themselves with the added dimension of being
able to use the computer's sound, graphic, and text capabilities to enrich their
ad or commercial. When completed, the youngster will be able to print a hard
copy of the ad or commercial and could use it as a focal point of discussion with
the therapist. Over time, a series of ads, or a "campaign," can be used to both
monitor and push therapeutic progress. It is exciting to watch the youngsters
involved in this activity open up and begin to explore the various facets of their
problems and personality as they construct the ads. It is valuable for reinforcing
their strengths, and an especially effective rapport-building activity for adolescents who are initially unwilling to communicate with the therapist, and who
often feel "put down" by the counseling process.

▶ Time Frame for the Activity

You should plan on working on this activity over a minimum of a three- to four-
session time frame if you want to focus on home, school, and friend contexts.
However, a single ad, or a long series, can also be used.

▶ Clinical Rationale

Making a commercial or ad involves selling a product. It involves focusing on
what is good about something, rather than what is bad. It involves focusing on
what is desirable, rather than what is not. Turning this technique toward children and adolescents allows them to creatively explore their feelings and opin-
ions about themselves in different contexts. It allows you to find sources of
strength upon which to build. Having children create commercials or print ads

about themselves provides a tangible, concrete way for children to express their feelings that otherwise might be difficult to verbalize. It gives you great insight into the self-perception of a client in relationship to significant others, their academic setting, and their peer relationships. This activity can point to areas where change is needed, and provides a tool to see progress in the "self-selling" process.

▶ *Developmental Considerations*

Sometimes it is helpful to start by asking children to bring in samples of ads, or by having magazines in your office for kids of varying ages so you can show them what you mean. Children with little or no typing skills can dictate what they want typed. Give the child options to modify color, font, size, and style of printed text. Preadolescents and older children are likely to need little help with this activity.

Note: This is an excellent activity for adults as well, especially for parents and teachers to create print ads or commercials for children who are giving them a difficult time. Relatedly, it is useful for parents and teachers to reacquaint themselves with their own strengths in dealing with children.

MINIMUM MATERIALS	OPTIONAL MATERIALS	THERAPEUTIC APPLICATIONS
AppleWorks, Microsoft Office, Kid Pix Studio	scanner, digital camera, sound clips, clip art	Identity issues, peer conflicts, family conflicts, depression, school problems, issues surrounding sexuality, physical abuse, sexual abuse, parent-child conflicts, and authority issues.

▶ *Preparing the Child*

It is important for you to prepare the child for this activity and explain what is to be accomplished. Take the time to discuss the concept of advertisements and show how it is applied in practice in magazines and newspapers. Explain that in the world of advertisement, the purpose of an ad is to sell an idea or product. In this activity, the goal is for the child to show a positive side of him- or herself that may not be shown very often. You will want to have advertisements handy so that there can be a discussion of what they are attempting to accomplish by the ad. Focus on the visual representation, the text, and how the advertiser helps to sell the concept, idea, or product. After beginning with positive ads, you might want to bridge into classified ads—help wanted ads to enable the child to communicate conflicts and concerns in the context of an advertisement. Have a paper and pencil handy as you brainstorm possible focal points with the child, which might be depicted or conveyed in the advertisement, and possible formats for the ads.

This technique is applicable to many children and adolescents who may be hesitant to reveal their conflicts about issues relating to home, school, and friends. By getting the child involved in creating an advertisement about the various settings in which he or she interacts, you will gain further insight into the youngster's conflicts and unresolved issues. Having children work in an "ad" mode engages them in a creative and non-threatening manner and allows them to select those parts of their lives they are ready to share with you. From a clinical perspective, the advertisement can be considered and used in ways consistent with various theoretical points of view. In what is chosen and not chosen, how it is portrayed, the affective tone, the stresses and coping strategies employed, and the self-definition of personal print ads, especially as they resolve over time, much rich personal material becomes available. This set of activities allows the computer to become a key clinical tool in helping children communicate their deepest concern, without necessarily using interpersonal verbal expression as the primary modality. It helps children identify strengths they are overlooking for a variety of emotional reasons.

GETTING STARTED

❶ If the student will be creating a print advertisement, open up AppleWorks and select Drawing Document.

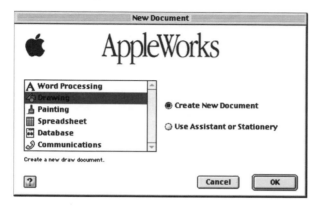

❷ From the File Menu, select Page Setup.

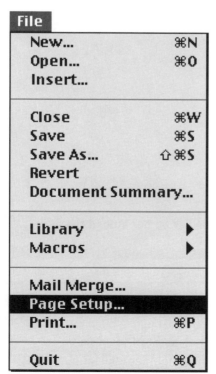

❸ Select Landscape Mode from the dialog box.

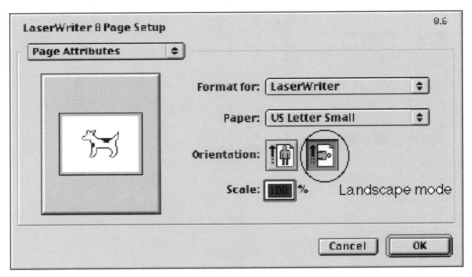

❹ Click on the Zoom Percentage Box and select 50% view.

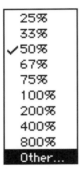

❺ Select the rectangle tool and draw a rectangular border around the edge of the page.

6 With the 4 handles of the rectangle still visible, select Lock from the Arrange Menu. This will lock the border in place.

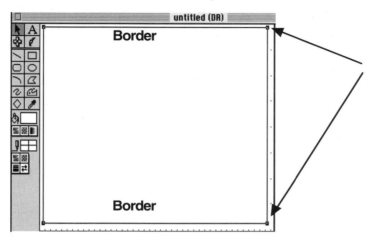

7 Now that the preliminary work has been done, you are ready to have the child create an advertisement or commercial about him or herself. Remember, sound clips and clip art from the library are resources that can be accessed. Having a mix of sound and graphic elements increases the child's engagement in the activity.

8 To add a heading for the advertisement, click on the Text Tool, and then click on the page. You will notice that a text box appears, waiting for you to type some text. Since you will want to bring attention to the text, select 36 point from the Size Menu before you begin typing. If you want to follow a template for practice, have the child type "My Life in the Burbs." Otherwise, have the child insert a title.

Text Tool

Remember, you can spell check your advertisement by going under the Edit Menu and selecting Writing Tools and then selecting Check Document Spelling.

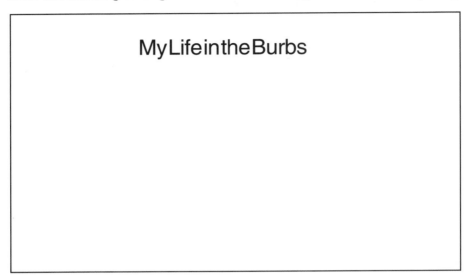

MyLifeintheBurbs

9 Go under the File Menu and select Library. Select Community and place a copy of the house on top of the page to give the student a focal point. To add pictures from the stored libraries, select the Library Command from the File Menu. This will allow you to select from one of the built in libraries of Clip Art. Select the Community library to open it.

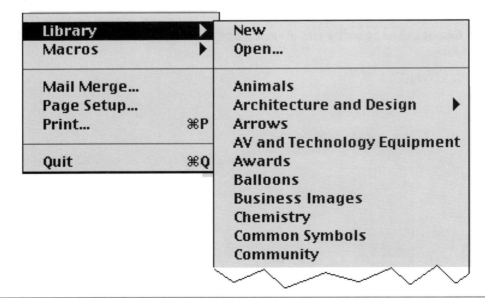

The student can quickly select and drag the house from the library and add it to the ad.

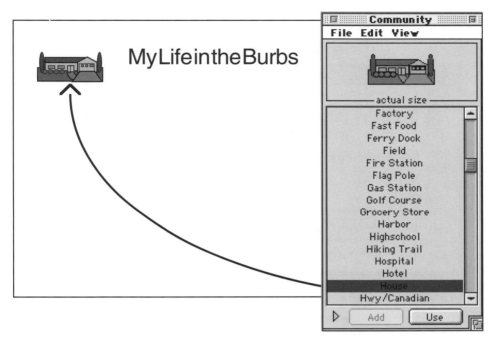

⑩ Have the child use the word processor to type some copy about his/her home. At this time, you may want to cue or prompt the child to think about various positive aspects of life at home as a jumping off point.

⑪ One of the exciting parts of this activity is the ability to add sound to the advertisement. Using a sound clip library, which is commercially available, the child could add sound to the advertisement. To add a sound to the advertisement, go to the File Menu and select Insert. When the dialog box appears, select a sound file that is stored on your hard disk and click the Insert button.

⓬ Once you have completed this step, you will notice that a small sound clip icon now appears on your page. Double click on it to hear the sound.

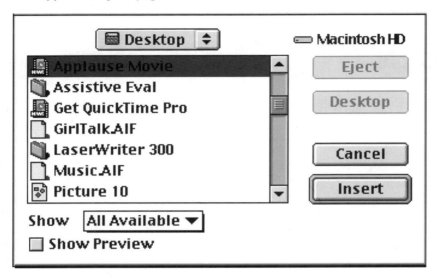

Use a Quick Cam to create a small video that can be integrated into the advertisement. Have the youngster use the Quick Cam to digitize pictures of his or her family into the advertisement.

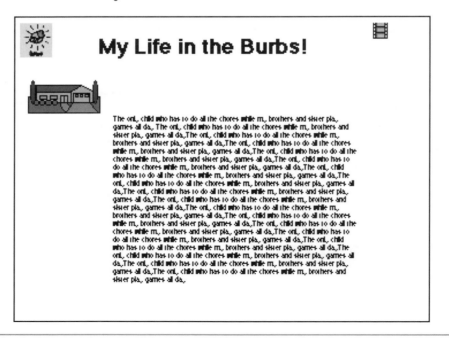

CLINICAL CASE ILLUSTRATION

Steve was a sixteen-year-old youngster who was referred by his psychiatrist for therapy due to concerns about depression and a long-standing history of attentional problems. He was on stimulant medication and was not responding as hoped. Steve was in a high school setting and was frequently getting into arguments with his teachers. He often became oppositional when they made requests, and he spent considerable energy and time trying to embarrass them in front of the class.

When the therapist initially met Steve, he walked into the office with his jacket on, almost covering his head, as if to hide himself from the world. Steve was less than communicative and did not understand why his parents had taken him to see the therapist. During the course of the interview, the therapist learned that Steve was a bright youngster who had a great deal of dislike for school and for teachers. Steve's parents expressed that their son was very down on himself, and there was concern about his level of self-confidence and self-esteem. When asked about strengths, the therapist learned that Steve had a facility with computers and enjoyed using one at home. With this as a backdrop, the therapist decided to use the *Create an Ad* activity with Steve to learn more about him, his difficulties, and conflicts.

Steve was hesitant to communicate his feelings and ideas directly with the therapist, but once he was put in front of the computer and it was explained what he was to do, he became very engaged in the activity. (As an aside, it is important that the therapist is facilitating the therapeutic activity, even if the adolescent appears to be able to do it on his or her own. This assists with rapport building and showing a genuine interest in the activity at hand.) Based on the presenting problem, and thinking that Steve would be more willing to create an ad about school, the therapist started with this activity first. The therapist asked Steve to create an ad about himself in school. The therapist gave Steve some examples of ads

CLINICAL CASE ILLUSTRATION

from television and from the print media to use as a guidepost and then set him up in front of the computer to create his ad. The therapist showed Steve how to access the clip art in the Library and how to use some of the graphic tools that were available in AppleWorks.

The therapist noted that Steve enjoyed the freedom he had to use the computer and quickly became engaged in the activity. Steve approached the task by first looking at the clip art that he had available to him. Once he reviewed the clip art, his eye caught a picture of a teacher in front of the classroom instructing her students. He proceeded to type a homework list on the blackboard and with heavy black lines crossed it out. The therapist noted spelling errors and was speculating whether the youngster may have a concomitant learning disability in addition to the presenting problems that were noted at the time of the referral. During the time that Steve was engaged in the activity, the therapist recorded some observations that he would need to follow up on after Steve completed the ad. Steve went on to add graphic text to his ad, which expressed both how he felt about school and teachers. He used text to state how he was feeling when sitting in the classroom, and his style depicted a great deal of anger. He labeled his drawing "Big Man on Campus," which should give you an idea about he felt about himself, even though he was a youngster of small stature. His finished product is included here to review. This advertisement led to some very interesting discussions about his school history, learning difficulties, and his feelings about himself at school.

From the advertisement, the therapist could quickly tell that school was a source of extreme frustration for Steve. The therapist, in a supportive and reflective manner, stated this to Steve. With little urging or prompting, Steve became more animated and began to share with the therapist how he felt about school and how, at a young age, he found learning to be difficult. He shared that in the second grade, other kids began making fun of him because he couldn't read or write well. This continued until third grade, when he shared that he was tested and found to have a learning disability. Steve did share that he has made a lot of progress in his reading and writing, but it still doesn't come easy for him. He did wish that his teachers were more understanding of his learning disability and did not always attribute his lack of progress to being lazy and unmotivated. The therapist found this activity to be quite enlightening and opened the doors for Steve to be able to talk about his frustration in school.

The therapist decided to next have Steve create a print ad about his interests and hobbies as a means of self-discovery. Steve was initially reluctant, but the therapist sat down in front of the computer and began to show him all of the various clip art he had available to him. The picture of the motorcycle really captured his interest, and Steve decided to give it a try. Steve explained to the therapist that he had been riding for some time now

CLINICAL CASE ILLUSTRATION

on his parents' property and really enjoyed the sense of freedom he experienced while driving. He expressed that some day he would love to race competitively and could see himself winning many trophies. He then went on to explore some of his other interests, which included using the computer. Steve pulled up the Library and began pasting a picture of a computer and a modem. He then went on the share with the therapist that he had become fascinated with telecommunications and had begun to teach himself how to do some programming, which he was proud of. While flipping through the other clip art libraries, he came to the sports library and quickly pasted a picture of a basketball. While he shared that he was not the best basketball player, he enjoyed the camaraderie of the other players and looked forward to playing games on the weekend. The therapist had learned a lot about Steve through this activity and had opportunities to reinforce his strengths and build on his self-confidence and esteem during the session.

Building Individual and Group Skills through Short Movies

SHORT MOVIES

GOAL

To have children explore various types of interactions as they are played out in groups.

▶ *Overview*

During this exercise, the youngster develops an interactive movie with scripting and animation. The youngster will have the capability to decide on the scene and then script the characters as they might appear in a real scenario, which gets played out time and time again. The youngster can select from over thirty different settings (e.g., arcade, classroom, basketball game, and mall) in which to base his/her production. Once the setting has been selected, the youngster will be able to select the cast of characters and decide on the sound effects, script, and actions of the characters. One unique aspect of the program is the capability to give the characters attributes that become integrated into how they carry out their script. Each member of the cast can say their lines using a different tone of voice (e.g., happy, angry, bored) which gives a real-life feel to the final production. Youngsters will enjoy the engaging quality of this task and in the process will learn more about themselves and the social dynamics of being a member of a group.

Hollywood High is an example of a software application that gives children the capability to be the director of their own movie, complete with background, characters, sound effects, and the script. Hollywood High was selected for clinical use for several reasons. First, Hollywood High is cross-platform and will work on either a Macintosh or Windows computer. Second, it is both inexpensive and easy to use and has clinical applications across a wide spectrum of problem areas. Before you get started working with Hollywood High, you may want to brainstorm some situations or scenarios that could be used with typical cases one might be working with. In some instances, it may be helpful for you to set up situations and have the youngster complete the script. Throughout, help children keep the perspective of being the director. This allows you to ask them to explore options at many points in the work, to explain their decisions, and to take responsibility.

▶ *Time Frame for the Activity*

Hollywood High lends itself to being used in many ways by the clinician. It is common to spend one to two sessions just developing a Hollywood High movie. A brief movie could be completed in a subsequent session. However, children and adolescents with good computer skills will find this a very engaging activity, and it is likely that the use of the program will span multiple sessions and can be open-ended.

▶ *Clinical Rationale*

Children are often times unaware of the group dynamics that play havoc on their social lives. Many of the children and adolescents that are in counseling are often there because they lack friendships or don't get along well when they are placed into group settings. Using software that allows for the development of scripts and role-playing can expand the repertoire of social skills and allow youngsters the capability to view their behavior in the context of social interactions. This activity provides a unique opportunity for the clinician to get a clearer understanding of the youngster's social skills as portrayed in various social settings.

▶ *Developmental Considerations*

It should be pointed out that there are several levels of use of the program, depending on the child's age, cognitive abilities, and language skills. As an entry-level use of the program, the therapist can set up scenarios and have the child modify one aspect of the scene (i.e., the dialog, body posture, or action). Moving up a level, the therapist selects certain parameters of the movie, such as the type of interaction (i.e., between school mates, parent-child). The child can then fill in who and when. At the third level, the therapist and the child can plan a script from the beginning and add the setting and characters as seen fit. These activities are very engaging and add a wealth of clinical information to work through with the child during a counseling session.

Generally, it is recommended that Hollywood High be used with children ages nine and up. Younger students may have a difficult time relating to the teenage characters. However, by calling the company, Grolier Interactive, who publishes

Hollywood High, you can access the program Hollywood, which uses a set of animal-like characters. Younger children tend to relate to these characters better, especially if they have no older siblings.

MINIMUM MATERIALS	OPTIONAL MATERIALS	THERAPEUTIC APPLICATIONS
Hollywood High	Hollywood (earlier version of Hollywood High)	identity issues, peer conflicts, depression, school problems, child-authority conflicts, social anxiety, social approach skills, conversational skills, cooperative activities

▶ *Preparing the Child*

It is important for you to become somewhat acquainted with Hollywood High before using it with children. Going through the tutorial and the manual should take less than sixty minutes and will give you the confidence to use it with children in clinical and counseling contexts.

One of the key concepts of directing a movie is that of the storyboarding progress that takes place. Some blank storyboards are provided at the end of the chapter and should be used before the child gets in front of the computer. Storyboarding allows the clinician and the child to discuss the type of movie that is going to be put together and assists the child in thinking through the story line and flow of the interaction.

For diagnostic purposes, you may allow children to develop their own movies with little initial guidance or structure. This type of activity can be very revealing and point out some underlying conflicts and problematic areas. However, if there are particular social-interpersonal situations that clearly are causing difficulty, you may be more inclined to create some scenarios with Hollywood High beforehand and then have the child complete the scenes. This will give you some insight into how the child may choose to resolve certain social problems in the context of the computer application.

Similarly, before you get started working with Hollywood High, you may want to brainstorm some situations or scenarios that could be used while working with the software. You and the child can spend time storyboarding the scenario and then put it into action and discuss the possible outcomes. This program gives you a great deal of latitude in helping the child look at various social situations from different angles and perspectives. It is also useful for you to have at your disposal to work with adolescents on body language and intonation. Since many of the youth that we work with often are not sensitive to non-verbal cues, this is an area that can be focused on using this software program. Set up various scenarios in advance and have the child respond by playing out the roles using varying forms of body language and intonation. Once children learn how their behaviors may not be appropriate to the situation, they can role-play the scenarios with you directly.

Finally, you probably will want to prepare some Hollywood High movies to show the child what the final outcome of the activity will be. For younger children, showing them simple and less complex movies will suffice. For adolescents, more complex movies can be viewed to demonstrate the technicalities of the finished movie. This will lead right into a discussion of the topic and theme that they would like to develop. While this activity involves more preparation than most others in this book, the power and flexibility of the program for simulating group contexts is well worth the investment.

GETTING STARTED

For the purpose of demonstration, we will take you step by step through a particular application of the Hollywood High program. We will outline a situation to use to introduce Hollywood High to a child and create a sample movie. Then you and the child can work off this example and modify it or start from the beginning. Regardless, the first step is storyboarding to select characters and backgrounds and plan the script. Use the blank template, which can be found on page 113, to work through the example with a child.

1 Storyboard the scene by putting down ideas for the setting, characters, and the interaction among the players. Here is an example:

Story Boarding for Hollywood High

Characters: Gary, Bobby, Amy, Glenn, Susan
Setting: The Movie Theater
Theme: Unsure what to say in social situations.
Feelings: shy, uncomfortable, nervous

Description of Scene
Gary and Bobby meet up with some friends unexpectedly at the movie theater and are surprised. They are not sure what to say or do.

Storyboarding a Scene for Hollywood High

2 Working off the basic situation we have provided, spend some time talking with the youngster about the script and what his or her friends might say or do in this situation. You may want to jot down the ideas as you discuss them so that when you are ready to use them in the program, you can do so. Remember that you are using this as a clinical tool and will gain much insight into the child's thinking, as well as learn more about how they would resolve this uncomfortable situation even if it is not a focal problem. Here is an example of some scripting that can be done. Use this script as is, present it and modify it, or create a new one.

3 Once you have storyboarded the scene and have developed the script, it is now time to put Hollywood High to work for you. To begin, double click on the Hollywood High icon to start the program.

Hollywood High Icon

❹ You will be presented with the opening Hollywood High screen where you will be able to select the settings and the characters. Select the movie lobby by double clicking on the picture of the movie lobby. If the movie setting is not in the first group of settings, use the up and down arrows to view additional settings.

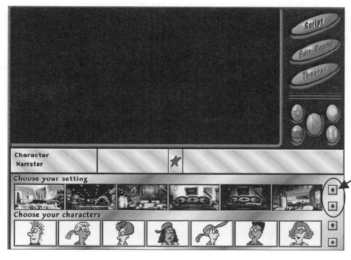

Opening Screen of Hollywood High

❺ After you have selected the movie lobby setting, your screen should look like this:

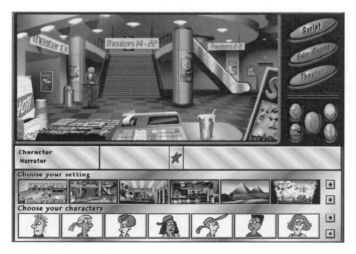

Movie Theater Lobby

6 Choose the following characters from the bottom of the screen by double clicking on them. Use up and down arrows to view additional characters for your scene.

7 Choose the following characters from the bottom of the screen by double clicking on the picture.

Since you want to model a situation that the child is familiar with, it is important to consider gender, ethnic, and personality characteristics that best match the child you are working with and his or her peers.

8 When you have done this, your screen should have characters in this scene. Notice that the character called Gary is outlined in green. This is the way the program lets us know that a character has been selected so that we can change some of the attributes.

We have now accomplished two things. We have selected the setting for the interaction and selected the characters.

We will now use the topmost menu bar to set the attributes for each character.

To change the name of the character and to personalize Gary's attributes, click on the red star. When you have done this, you will see the following screen.

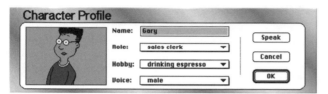

Using the character profile screen, you can change Gary's name, role, hobby, and the sound of his voice. (For the purpose of demonstration, we suggest leaving his name as is.) To check out the various voice sounds, just select the speak button that is located in the Character Profile screen. When you are done making your changes, click on the OK button or hit the Return key.

9 To change how Gary is feeling, click on the pull down button to reveal a list of various feeling states. After you have selected "happy," notice how the facial features change. Go down the list and experiment with the various emotional states that each character can experience. In this instance, the script says that Gary is feeling rather surprised, so select this feeling state.

⑩ Use the following icons to pose Gary in the scene. With Gary selected (green outline showing), click on each icon to pose him differently. If you need to turn him around in a scene, just click on the red arrow. Select the first picture showing Gary's body language and expression to be somewhat surprised. Now go back and select the other characters and select their body postures and feeling states to match the storyboarding.

With the setting and the character selected, it is now time to begin to type in the script that was developed when you were doing your storyboarding. Hollywood High gives you the capability to link several settings together and to add characters as you need them.

⑪ To begin writing a script for the scene, click on the Script button on the screen.

Hollywood High will now display the following screen with the top half of the screen showing the setting and bottom half showing the script window.

⑫ To give Gary an action, just click on the Action button on the screen. When you have clicked on the button, the Actions dialog box will appear and then you can select an action for Gary. To make Gary stare, just select the stare action. For your reference, a list of actions appears at the end of this chapter.

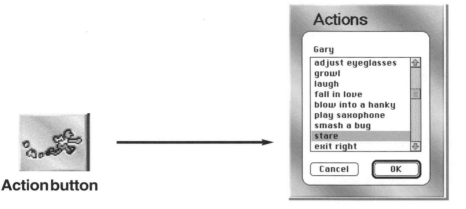

Action button

🔹 To give the character another action just select the Action button again and select another action. You will notice in the script window that Gary's actions are spelled out in parentheses.

Script Window

🔹 To have Gary act out his part, begin to type in the script. Place your cursor after the actions and begin to type in what you would like Gary to say. Refer back to your storyboard. For example, "What are you doing here?"

Script Window

⑮ To add other characters to the scene, just click on the Edit Scene button, which will take you to the Main Menu screen. Click on Glenn to add him to the scene. To move Glenn to the center of the scene, click and drag him to the position you desire. You will notice that the cursor changes to a hand so that he can be moved.

⑯ Click on the Script button to enable you to give Glenn his script. Click on the Action button to select an action for Glenn. For example, you could have him eating a hot dog and looking surprised as he dialogs with Gary. Now type, "I thought I told you we were coming to the movies!" Now that you have the basics down, you can add other characters to the scene with text and actions. When you are done, your script and included actions in parentheses should look something like this:

Gary: Hey, what are you guys doing here?
John: What do you mean?
Gary: You didn't tell us you were going to the movies!
Bobby: (Looking uncomfortable and meek) Right!
Amy: Well, we decided to see the movie at the last moment.

⑰ Let's add a title to our movie. Click on the Title button. When you have done this, a dialog box appears. Type into the title box, "A Night at the Movies," and have the title appear for 4 seconds. When you are done, click the OK button.

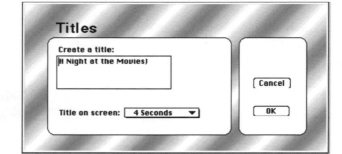

⑱ To quickly view what you have done up until this point, click on the green, triangular button. This will run your movie and show you how the characters are interacting on the screen.

To see the entire movie being run in the theater, click on the Theater button.

After you have clicked on the Theater button, you will be taken to a new view of your movie. To see your movie run in its entirety, just click on the green, triangular button and watch the movie roll.

With the basics laid out, it is now time to explore ways to use this program with clients.

▶ *Clinical Consideration*

Hollywood High is appropriate to use for children who have social skills deficits or are having difficulty working in groups and understanding cause and effect. In order to work on social skills deficits, it can be most efficient to use this program to set up some scenarios and then have children complete the script and the actions for the characters. This adds a great deal to the session and can be used as a jumping off point for discussion about all of the possible outcomes of the interaction. Just having the capacity to change the actions of the characters could lead to a discussion about how one interprets body language and how to use facial features to discern how the other person is feeling. In our experience, the program comes closest to simulating key aspects of social situations in an individual treatment context. However, using the program in a social skills group is another powerful application, once you have mastered it with individual children.

CLINICAL CASE ILLUSTRATION

Bobby was an eleven-year-old youngster who was referred to therapy due to concerns about poor social skills and a long-standing history of attentional problems. Bobby had recently entered middle school and was having a difficult time making friends and working in small group activities. Several of his teachers were concerned about his inability to pick up on social cues and difficulties with effective problem solving without an adult present. Bobby was frequently getting into fights and arguments with his peers and could not figure out why he had no friends in his grade. By all accounts, most of the other children were tired of Bobby's antics and wanted nothing to do with him. Bobby was having a difficult time understanding this, and, the more he tried to befriend his classmates, the worse it became. It was at this point that Bobby's parents decided to begin therapy.

When the therapist initially met Bobby, he walked into the office, looked all around, and began to poke around on the therapist's desk, picking up items. Bobby quickly started asking the therapist a lot of questions. The therapist noted that Bobby was an incessant talker and in many ways had a hard time understanding personal space and boundaries. This proved to be a critical piece of the puzzle and one that would need to be addressed during the therapy. Although Bobby was extremely communicative, he tended to be very internally driven, based on his needs. Often, Bobby could not follow along with the discussion and tended to easily get off target and change the topic of conversation. The therapist noted this and now had a better understanding of how his communication style would interfere with his development of friendships.

After four sessions, the therapist learned that Bobby was a lonely youngster who wanted to be liked by the other children in school. The therapist realized early on that Bobby would benefit from some individual therapy sessions as well as being part of a group where he could work on his social

CLINICAL CASE ILLUSTRATION

skills. With this as a backdrop, the therapist decided to use Hollywood High with Bobby to help him focus on his social skills and on how he might interact with other children his own age. The therapist decided to set up some scenarios before the session and have Bobby respond as though he were one of the characters in the script. Here is a step-by-step approach to creating this type of activity.

The therapist shared with Bobby that one of the things they were going to be concentrating on during the session was his social skills. The therapist stated that he knew Bobby badly wanted to form friendships with the other children and that some of the activities on the computer would help him learn not only what to say but how to say it.

1 **Select a setting. In this case the school gym was used as the setting for the scenario.**

School Gym Setting

CLINICAL CASE ILLUSTRATION

2 Next, we added some children to the scene to create an opportunity for them to interact. We added Matt, Gary, and Lily to the scene by clicking on them in the Character Menu Bar.

3 In this scenario, we had Bobby in the role of Matt, who is furthest to the left in the scene. The script will go something like this:

Lilly and Gary are planning to go out to eat after the basketball game and select a place that Matt is not fond of. Matt's feeling state was set to reflective from the pull down menu. Both Lilly and Gary's feeling state was set to happy.

4 The script was now set up to have Bobby play the role of Matt, who is looking a little upset. By clicking on the Script button, we could develop the script for the characters. In this scenario, the therapist put Matt into the script but left out what he said. Here is an example of the script that was used.

CLINICAL CASE ILLUSTRATION

SCENE: In the Basketball Gym

(SFX: basketball gym) {Special sound effect}

GARY: (Gary adjusts eyeglasses.) Hi Lilly. Did you enjoy the game?

LILLY: (Lilly giggles.) I certainly did. Our school team played very well tonight. Hey, Matt. What do you think?

MATT:

GARY: They certainly did. Did you see the way Charles played today?

MATT:

LILLY: It looks like we will get into the play-offs.

MATT:

GARY: It certainly does.

LILLY: You know, I am getting hungry. What do you say we go to Main Street Diner?

GARY: That sounds great!

MATT:

❺ Before Bobby began to work on the task, the therapist discussed with him the scenario that he would be working on. By giving him a context for the scenario, it made it easier for Bobby to come up with the social language that he needed to respond to this task. The therapist and Bobby talked about the goal of using Matt to show how Bobby would respond to the scenario. Next, Hollywood High was opened to the school gym scenario. Bobby played the role of Matt, adding what he would say given the situation that had been set-up and also Matt's actions.

The therapeutic activity is an example of one that is easy to set up and has great clinical utility. The present example used the program diagnostically with the therapist mainly creating the scenario and then having the child complete it without much discussion or input. From this, changes were made in the scenario on the computer to see what worked better. Finally, the therapist and Bobby role-played to see if it works. In this case, and generally, it is important to reflect back to the child what his goal is. If the goal is to make more friends, then one needs to point out that all of the social language and overt behaviors should support and facilitate pro-social behavior. During the role playing, the therapist stopped at key points in the discourse and had the child reflect on the choices that were made during the scenario. The therapist then joined with the child to help him problem solve ways that might be more effective in helping him reach the desired goal.

Bobby was a good candidate to use the computer, and the therapist explained to him that they would work together to try to help him solve his social problems. The therapist pointed out that while Bobby wanted the other children to accept him, he was not always approaching them in a manner that was allowing him to accomplish that. The therapist shared with Bobby that the computer activity would allow him to test out different ways to solve the problem. After working with Bobby for a few sessions, using the diagnostic example presented above, the therapist decided to begin to work on the following skills with Bobby:

- **Understanding facial features and body language**
- **Staying on topic**
- **Keeping a conversation going**

Using Hollywood High, the therapist began to create some new scenarios that would allow Bobby to comment on the interactions and allow him to write the scripts to some of the storylines that were created by the therapist. In the first activity, the therapist decided that it was extremely important that Bobby be better grounded in his ability to identify the feelings of others on the basis of their facial expressions. The therapist talked with Bobby about body language and non-verbal communication and just how important a role it plays in day-to-day interactions. During the session, Bobby and the therapist role-played, and Bobby had to figure out how the therapist might be feeling based on his body language. After this, the therapist selected some of the male and female characters from Hollywood High and gave each character one of the following feeling states: sad, angry, happy, and shy. The therapist also set up each character in a different pose so as to reflect different body posturing. Again, the purpose of this activity was for Bobby to begin to identify the feeling state of each character so as to help sensitize him about his interaction with others. One of the key steps in resolving social problems is to identify one's own feelings and those of others. The therapist used the screen below to have a discussion about how each of the characters might be feeling and what the key discriminating features are that would clue Bobby into this.

Activity One

Therapist: Bobby, please take a look at the characters starting from the left and tell me how you think they are feeling. Also, tell me some clues that let you know how they are feeling.

Bobby: OK, but what do you mean by clues?

Therapist: Clues are what give you some ideas about how they are feeling. Remember, we spoke about looking at facial features and also body posture as clues to let us know how someone may be feeling.

Bobby: Now I understand! The girl on the left looks a little confused or may be a little upset. Her hands are on her hips and eyes are open wide.

Therapist: Very good, Bobby. Now you get the idea. You said her hands were on her hips. What does that tell you?

Bobby: I think that maybe she was annoyed or something.

The therapist continued to have Bobby look at the other characters and have him reveal how he thought the others were feeling. This activity sensitized Bobby as to the importance of non-verbal cues. It also showed him to look at these features in the course of his daily interactions. This activity was a real stimulus for Bobby to begin to identify and realize just how important it was to figure out how his friends might be feeling during an interaction. This activity generated a great deal of discussion, as the therapist was able to point out the various aspects of the facial features that give us clues as to how others are feeling. Bobby enjoyed the activity and was put at ease by focusing on the characters on the computer screen and not talking about his peers and their reactions, which may have been too close to home. The therapist was also able to begin to focus on the characters' body language. Looking at each of the characters, the therapist was able to have a discussion about how the characters' body language was conveying meaning that was important to recognize during interpersonal interactions.

The therapist spent some time during the course of the next couple of sessions to help Bobby identify others' feelings and how to approach and use reflective listening skills as part of his repertoire of interpersonal skills. The therapist explained to Bobby that there would be times when it would be important to be able to learn more about how others are feeling. One of the ways to do this was by using a technique called reflective listening. Bobby had never heard that term before and listened intently to the therapist. During the session, the therapist modeled what reflective listening sounded like and had Bobby try to emulate him. While Bobby found this to be initially rather awkward, by the end of the session he was able to get the hang of it. At the end of the session, Bobby got some homework. He was asked to use the reflective listening skills with his parents in his home and to report back what had happened when he did so.

In activity two, the therapist wanted to see what Bobby had learned from their discussions and decided to set the stage for Bobby to add the script, but with one caveat. He had to use the reflective listening skills he had been practicing when he worked on the program. With this activity, the therapist was able to evaluate what Bobby had learned and find out if he was capable of focusing on the body language and facial cues to help piece together the reflective dialog. The therapist had Bobby take the perspective of one of the characters in the setting and had to use reflective skills to communicate how the character was feeling. In the example below, Bobby was asked to take the perspective of the character on the left and to make a reflective statement about how the person on the right might be feeling. Bobby added the following script for activity two.

Activity Two

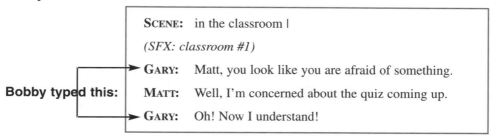

Bobby typed this:

> **SCENE:** in the classroom |
>
> *(SFX: classroom #1)*
>
> **GARY:** Matt, you look like you are afraid of something.
>
> **MATT:** Well, I'm concerned about the quiz coming up.
>
> **GARY:** Oh! Now I understand!

Script for Activity Two

The therapist was delighted to see that Bobby could identify the feeling state and was beginning to focus on how the other person was feeling, instead of always focusing on his needs first. This activity, repeated with other examples, was extremely engaging for Bobby and helped him to understand the skills that were necessary for him to become a more effective communicator.

As Bobby and the therapist began working together, the therapist decided to use Hollywood High to help Bobby learn how to keep on topic when having a conversation. The therapist had observed, during his interaction with Bobby, that keeping on the conversational topic was a difficult task for him. Rather than initially focusing directly on this as a problem with Bobby, the therapist decided that it would be to his advantage if he could put some emotional distance between the problem and his client. It would be easier to talk about the problem in the abstract using the Hollywood High characters as opposed to being direct about the problem with Bobby. The therapist, therefore, decided to set up a scenario whereby there were four characters in the scene having a conversation about the annual community fair, which was coming into town on the weekend. The three characters on the right of the screen would be having a conversation about the fair, keeping on the topic. The character on the extreme left would consistently talk off topic.

This proved to be a very interesting activity. The therapist asked Bobby to be an observer and watch what happened during the interaction. After the scene was completed, the therapist asked Bobby to describe what happened and how the individuals interacted with each other. Bobby was quick to point out that the character on the left was off topic and not really included in what the others were talking about. He also noted her glum reaction.

This activity was repeated, along with homework assignments to notice conversations among peers and then to monitor his own ability to stay on topic. In addition, the parents were asked to help monitor and prompt this. Reflective listening became a tool that was used often. Gradually, the focus of treatment shifted to role-plays and the in-vivo homework assignments. But, in this case, as with many others, Hollywood High served as a vital therapeutic bridge and instructional tool. Bobby's social skills improved, and he began gaining acceptance among his school peers.

Interaction Scene

Generally speaking, Hollywood High is very versatile in helping to address the social and emotional needs of children and adolescents. The program has many sophisticated features that allow those with whom you are working to cast full-length movies, complete with multiple backgrounds and actors. As noted earlier, for younger children, Hollywood High offers a feature whereby, for a small fee, you can have access to animal characters and additional backgrounds to integrate into your movies.

Over time, you will accumulate a library of Hollywood High scenarios that you can view with a child during a session. It is not often that we can observe kids' reactions and the steps they might take at correcting different situations. This provides us with an insight into the child, which we rarely get a glimpse at, outside of our office setting. Think of the rich diagnostic material that can be gleaned from working with the child in this manner. And, think of using Hollywood High with parents, to see how well and accurately they know their child, how two parents might agree or disagree, and to clarify and identify areas of interpersonal effectiveness they believe their adolescent needs to improve.

SCENE: In the Suburbs

GARY: (Gary enters from offstage right) (Gary moves) Hello! What's going on?

MATT: (Matt faces right) We were just talking about the Fair that is coming into town next weekend. (Matt faces left)

JENNY: Wow! That sounds like fun! Were you thinking of going?

LILLY: Boy—School is really hard this year. (Lilly moves) (Lilly chews bubble gum)

GARY: (Gary looks happy) When would be the best time for us to go? (Gary moves)

MATT: (Matt faces right) (Matt looks happy) How about Friday night?

JENNY: (Jenny faces right) (Jenny points) (Jenny moves) Friday is good for me!

GARY: Friday night works for me!

LILLY: (Lilly looks silly) With school nearly over, what are you guys going to do this summer?

JENNY: (Jenny stares) (Jenny faces left)

Script for Interaction Scene

Airplane	Arcade	Basketball Game	Bathroom	Beach
Bowling Alley	Cafe	Cheerleaders' Gym	City Street	Classroom
Clothing Store	Comic Strip	Dance Gym	Eye of the Storm	Fast Food Counter
Garage	Haunted House	Leaning Tower	Living Room	Living Room at Night
Lookout Point	Mall	Movie Theater	Movies	Music Store
National Park	Orthodontist's Office	Pyramids	Locker Room	Silent Movie
Suburbs	Time Tunnel			

List of Background Settings in Hollywood High

happy	frightened	pompous	bored	flirtatious
sad	guilty	content	silly	shy
angry	paranoid	reflective	panicked	embarrassed
cool	confused	wistful	surprised	

List of Expressions for Characters in Hollywood High

Storyboarding Template

Description of Scene:

Description of Setting:

Characters to be Included:

Name:

Feeling

Action

Name:

Feeling

Action

Name:

Feeling

Action

Theme:

Personal Reflections on the Self

REFLECTIONS ON THE SELF

To have youngsters reflect on their past and present experiences and learn how they forge their identities.

▶ Overview

During this activity, children will develop a stack (the technical term for a group of related information that resemble computer index cards), which will allow them to reflect on their past experiences and present and future aspirations. This activity allows the youngster the capability to author their stack using graphics, sounds, and animation. If you have access to a digital camera, children can actually insert pictures of themselves into the stack. The children find this to be an engaging activity, while also progressively exploring facets of him/herself under your guidance. Like any other activity, a great deal of planning is needed to make it successful. Therefore, before the youngster actually gets on to the computer, you will explore and brainstorm ideas for the multimedia stack. Making the stack provides children with motivational incentives to look into their goals, aspirations, and conflicts.

This tool is especially useful when working with resistant adolescents that present with identity issues. What is fascinating about this activity is all the planning and discussion that must go on before the youngster ever goes on the computer to develop the stack. Use standard interview techniques and the storyboarding templates, which can be found at the end of the chapter.

You will be in a position to learn things about a child, which would take considerably longer using standard techniques. Additionally, the youngster comes into this therapeutic activity very excited and engaged, looking forward to creating a multimedia project that centers around who he/she is.

▶ Time Frame for the Activity

Clinicians should plan on working on this activity over a three- to four-session time frame. It can be open-ended and revisited periodically as therapy progresses.

▶ *Clinical Rationale*

Children are often times unaware of how their past and present experiences forge their identities. Many of the children and adolescents who are in counseling are often resistant to wanting to take a look at, or to reflect on, their past and their present conditions. At the heart of this exercise is the child's opening of him- or herself to the therapist and revealing a part of their identity and who they are. The youngster will also have an opportunity to project into the future and ponder what their lives might be like. Looking into the future allows the therapist to glimpse into the goals and values of the child without direct questioning. Using hypermedia software, the youngster can design an interactive multimedia stack using sound, graphics, animation, and text to work on this very engaging and enlightening activity.

▶ *Developmental Considerations*

To a large extent, the student's experience with computers may dictate what he/she can do independently. However, it is recommended that Hyperstudio be used with children ages 7 and older. The therapist may need to assist the younger child with reading the dialog boxes that appear on the screen. This is an ideal activity for the child who may be reticent or resistant to talking therapy. This activity is also well-suited for children who have attentional problems and who may find it difficult to talk while staying seated for long periods of time.

MINIMUM MATERIALS	OPTIONAL MATERIALS	THERAPEUTIC APPLICATIONS
Hyperstudio, iBuild, Multimedia Express, MPower	digital camera, scanner, clip art, sound files	Identity issues, peer conflicts, depression, school problems, issues surrounding parent-child conflicts, and authority.

GETTING STARTED

❶ **Double click on the Hyperstudio icon** **to start the program.**

❷ **You will then be presented with the following screen:**

Opening Screen of Hyperstudio

❸ **Click on the New Stack button on the bottom of the opening screen.**

④ You will be prompted with the following dialog box asking you whether you want to start a new stack. Select Yes.

This launches a new untitled stack. Are you sure you want to leave the Home Stack now?

No   Yes

⑤ You will be prompted with the next dialog box asking you if you want the same number of cards, color, and size for each new card in your stack. Go ahead and select Yes.

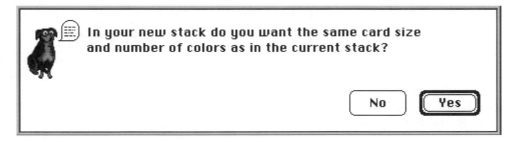

In your new stack do you want the same card size and number of colors as in the current stack?

No   Yes

⑥ When you have clicked on the Yes button, you will see a blank card, which is the building block of this application. Notice that the program automatically inserts the name of the stack and the card number in the title bar, in this case Untitled-Card 1.

Untitled – Card 1

Blank Card # 1

❼ To add a colored background to the card, select Erase Background from the Edit Menu. When the dialog box comes on the screen, select a background color for your card. It is usually best to stick with a light-colored background. Select a light gray background color for the first card.

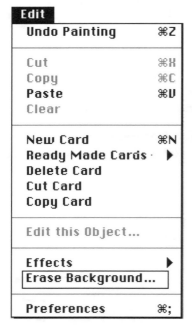

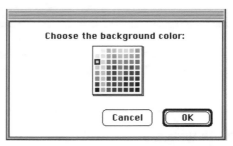

❽ Tear off the tool bar from the Tools Menu, and place it on the right side of the screen. Having the tool bar positioned on the screen will enable you to quickly access the tools that you will need.

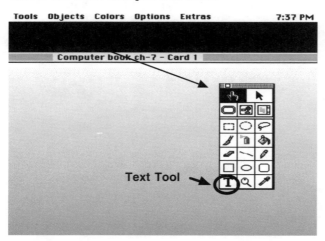

9 Using the Text Tool on the tool bar, title the first card "Reflections." Before we begin to type, choose a font and size for the lettering by selecting the Text Style from the Options Menu. Select Helvetica and choose a text color from the text color grid. Click OK when you are done. Now select the Text Tool and type on the screen "Reflections: Past, Present, and Future." Notice that after you select the text tool the cursor changes to a text "I" beam.

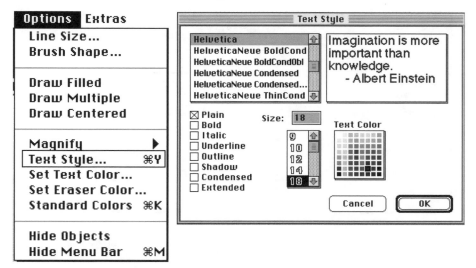

10 When you have completed this step, your card should look something like this:

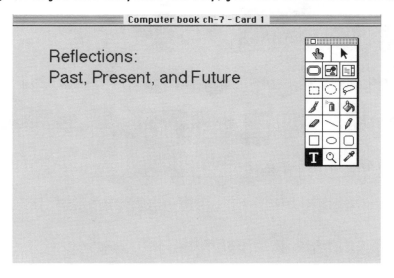

11 Add a picture to the first card. Select Add Clip Art from the File Menu. Select the file "Education 1" from your hard disk, which is located in the HS Art folder. After you have selected the file, you will be asked to select the graphic with the cross hair tool. Select the picture of the boy, and you will now notice that there are "marching ants" around the picture. Click OK and the graphic will be added to your card.

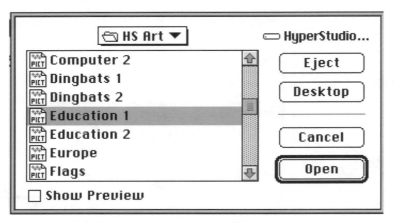

"Marching ants"

⑫ When you have completed this step, you will be able to position the graphic on the card. It should look something like this:

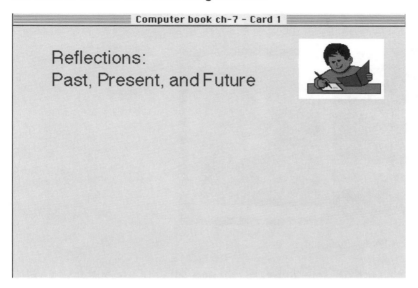

⑬ Create a new card to work on by selecting the New Card command from the Edit Menu. You will notice that Hyperstudio will automatically add the same background as you had selected for the first card. Since we are going to place a picture on this card, select a more appropriate background for the second card. Using the Import Background command from the File Menu, select the file "Album." Your second card should now look like this:

Use the Add Clip Art command to select the file "Aaron," which is located in the Family Pict folder. Use the cross hair tool to select the picture and click OK when you are done. Your second card should now look like this:

Card 2 with Photograph Added

⑭ To make this activity interactive, we are now going to use buttons to add sound and to help us navigate from one card to the next. To add a button, select Add a Button from the Objects Menu. This will bring up the Buttons Appearance dialog box, which allows you to control both how the button looks and behaves. In the Name Edit box, type "Back" and click on the OK button when you are done.

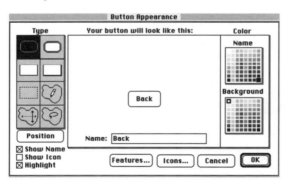

This brings up the Actions dialog box and allows us to define what the button does. Select Back. This button takes us back to the previous card. Click on the Icon button, and select the arrow pointing to the left. In this example, when we click on it, we will be taken back to Card 1. Position the button on the bottom left of the screen.

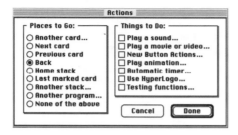

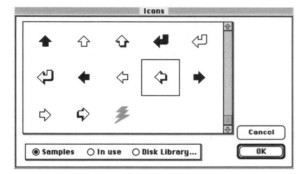

🕔 When you have completed these steps, your second card should look like this:

16 Now, add some text using the Add Text object command from the Object Menu to the left of the photograph. Select the Add Text Object from the menu, and the marching ant grid will appear on the screen. Position the text object to the left of the photograph and use the mouse to size the text object. Now you can type text into the text object as if you had a mini word processor.

17 Add some sound to the card to make it more interactive. To do this, create another button from the Objects Menu and place it on the card. Select Play a Sound from the Things to Do option on the right side of the dialog box. This brings up the Tape Deck dialog box. Type a name for the sound, click on the Record button, and begin to speak. When you are done, click on the OK button. When you go back to the card, click on the Speak button and hear what you recorded.

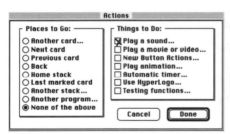

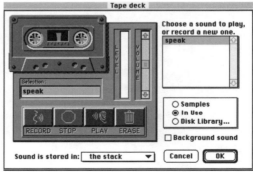

⓲ Add another button to navigate forward to another card. Refer back to the steps on how to create a button, and add the icon for the right pointed arrow. After you have accomplished this, your second card is complete and should look something like this:

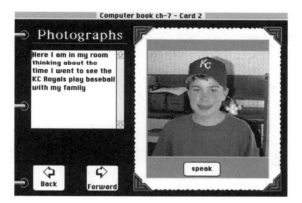

Congratulate yourself! You have learned a great deal in a short amount of time!

⓳ Add another card by going to the Edit Menu and selecting New Card. This card can be used to reflect the present experiences that the child would like to draw upon. Pictures of his/her family, friends, hobbies, likes, and dislikes can be explored. There is no limit to the number of cards that are used to create the stack. Using the storyboarding templates at the back of the chapter can assist in planning for the stack development. Add navigational arrows on the cards you have created so that you can effectively move from one card to the next. Using readily available clip art, you can create the third card to look something like this, which explores the child's present-day experiences and his/her interests. You can now use this card as a jumping off point so that when the child clicks on the music graphic it takes you to another card, which looks further into his/her musical interests.

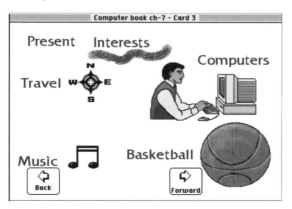

⑳ Create a new card and add navigational buttons. Add a button and name it "Music" in the dialog box. Position it on the bottom of the card. From the Things to Do option, select Play a Movie or Video and select the movie "Heat." You will now see the Quicktime Movies dialog box. Select Use Movie controller option and click OK. If you want to preview the video, click the Try It button.

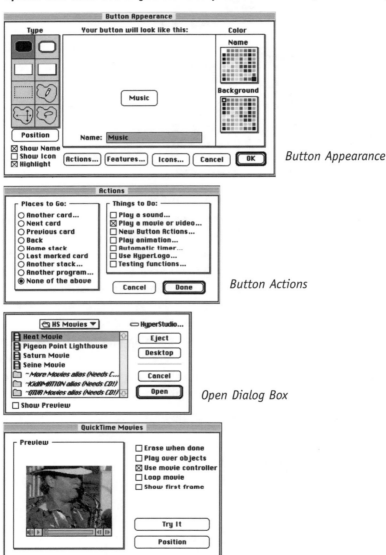

Button Appearance

Button Actions

Open Dialog Box

Quicktime Movies

21 When you have completed these steps, your card will look something like this:

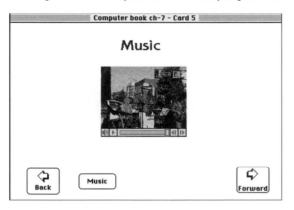

Click on the Music button to play the video.

22 Let's go back to Card 3, Present Interests, and link the musical note graphic to the movie. In order to do this, use the selection tool to select the musical graphic. Notice the marching ant border around the musical note. Go to the Object Menu and select Add a Graphic Object. When you do this, a dialog box will ask you if you want to change the selected item to a graphic object. Click on the Yes button.

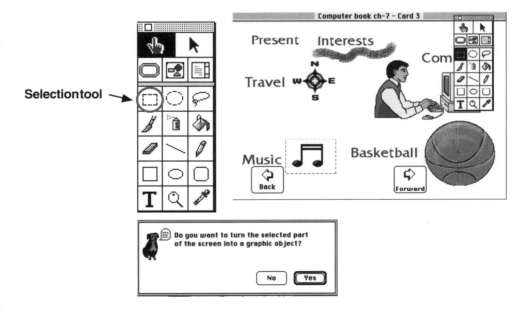

㉓ Now for the fun part! Let's link the musical note to the movie that you inserted into the stack. After you click on the Yes button, you will now be viewing the Graphic Appearance dialog box. Click on the Actions button to reveal the set of options. Under the Places to Go option, select Another Card. This brings up the Linking dialog box. Use the arrow keys to move to the card with the Quicktime video, and click on the OK button. Now when the youngster clicks on the musical note graphic, the program will go directly to the music video.

Graphic Appearance

Preview

Frame color

Features...

Actions...

Cancel

Frame width
0

☐ Disk based   Name: music note   OK

Actions

Places to Go:
◉ Another card...
○ Next card
○ Previous card
○ Back
○ Home stack
○ Last marked card
○ Another stack...
○ Another program...
○ None of the above

Things to Do:
☐ Play a sound...
☐ Play a movie or video...
☐ New Button Actions...
☐ Play animation...
☐ Automatic timer...
☐ Use HyperLogo...
☐ Testing functions...

Cancel   Done

Move to the card to connect to, then click OK.

◁   Cancel   OK   ▷

Tips:
    Type ⌘0 for connections to other stacks
    Type ⌘N if you need a new card

Computer book ch-7 - Card 6

Music

Move to the card to connect to, then click OK.

◁   Cancel   OK   ▷

Tips:
    Type ⌘0 for connections to other stacks
    Type ⌘N if you need a new card

◁ Back   Music   ▷ Forward

24 Create another card to have the youngster share what his/her perceptions are of the future. This is a very interesting facet of the activity and gives you insights into children's goals and aspirations. Here is an example of a card that one youngster created using Clip Art.

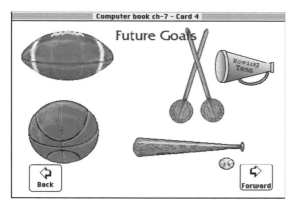

Important clinical issues to explore while using this hypermedia activity include the realism of recollections, present and future goals and aspirations, the breadth and nature of present and future goals, the match of these with parental and school expectations, the influences of sibling rivalry, and omissions in recollections, which might include denials when you bring up events you might know of from the historical case record.

CLINICAL CASE ILLUSTRATION

Jane was a thirteen-year-old youngster who was referred to counseling due to concerns about school performance and depression. Jane's parents had recently separated after being married for fifteen years. Jane rarely saw her father now, and there was a great deal of animosity between her parents over financial matters. Jane had always been a good student, and now the school was calling home to let her mother know that her grades were falling and that she was missing a great number of assignments. Jane's mother had noticed that she was spending more time in her room and that she wasn't spending as much time with her friends, whom she always seemed to enjoy. Jane's mom became concerned when Jane started to talk about how life wasn't worth living. When her

CLINICAL CASE ILLUSTRATION

mom questioned her more, she started to cry and reported to her mom that she had thoughts about taking her life. This prompted a quick referral to a therapist to help Jane deal with the changes in her family and with her depression.

When the therapist initially met Jane, she walked slowly into the office casting her eyes towards the ground. She sat next to her mother and spoke slowly and deliberately in a monotone voice with little emotion. Behind her eyes, the therapist could sense her pain and feelings of depression. Jane was quick to talk about her father and the recent separation but was unwilling to express her emotions. The therapist thought that using the reflections activity with multi-media software might help reveal more about Jane and help her be more willing to explore her feelings and the loss she was experiencing.

The therapist spent some time building rapport with Jane and then suggested that they try to work on the reflection activity. Jane had no idea what was involved in therapy but had taken some computer classes at school, which she enjoyed. Jane's curiosity was now piqued, and a certain spark was ignited when the therapist approached her about this interactive activity. The therapist explained the goal of the activity and shared that it would be helpful at first to do some talking and begin to work on the storyboarding before getting in front of the computer. The therapist's office was equipped with a digital camera and a scanner, which made it easy for Jane to bring in pictures and add them to the stack. Likewise, Jane could bring in some of her music CDs and could add music to the interactive stacks, which she was going to design. Jane was excited by the prospect of creating this work and looked forward to the next session.

At the next session, Jane and the therapist picked up where they left off. The therapist worked with Jane to complete the storyboarding before she started to work out her design on the computer. Jane was eager to talk to the therapist about her first card, which reflected a time in her life when

CLINICAL CASE ILLUSTRATION

she was feeling happy. She spoke about a time when she was ten years old and could remember playing on her computer in the family room with mom and dad in the house. The therapist was able to elicit a great deal of affect and could see that Jane must have been repressing a great deal during the time that her parents were separating. Jane spoke about all the good times that they had as a family, including the vacations, trips into town, and her parents watching her in the school band. Jane started to cry when she spoke about all of these experiences and thought that she could enter some of them onto her first card. Jane brought in a photograph of herself, which she scanned into the computer and placed in her stack. She then designed a text object and typed some text into the space provided. Jane thought that it would be great to add some speaking capabilities to the card and decided to record some of her moments while recording them onto the computer. She decided to create a button that would recount some of the happy moments in her family when she clicked on it.

Card 1: Happy Times

The therapist had noted the full range of emotions that Jane was experiencing and in their session had decided that it might be a good idea to storyboard a card about what she was experiencing. Jane was quick to

CLINICAL CASE ILLUSTRATION

identify with her sadness and noted that she was more moody, sullen, and angry as of late. The therapist asked her to reflect on these feelings and how she could convey them on her next card. They discussed it for awhile, and Jane decided that she would use some of the painting tools to express how she was feeling for her next card. Jane was highly engaged as she began to focus on the activity. She was able to release her feelings and talk more openly about what she was experiencing at home.

Card 2: My Feelings

While Jane was freer about expressing her feelings, the therapist guided the discussion towards the future and asked Jane to reflect on what it would look like for her. Jane made a big sigh and started to cry. She envisioned a picture of her parents together, but with her dad cut out of the picture. Certainly there were many issues to be worked through with Jane. However, the hypermedia reflection activity provided a valuable opportunity to engage this girl and gather therapeutic material in a non-threatening and efficient way. The cards that she created were referred to subsequently in therapy, with progress linked eventually to a more realistic, emotionally-accepted "future" card.

CLINICAL CASE ILLUSTRATION

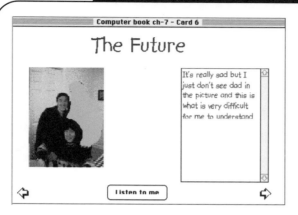

Card 3: The Future

Story boarding Template

Title of card	Description of Card

Background graphics   **Foreground graphics**

Navigational buttons   **Text fields**

Links   **Animation**

Storyboarding Template

Building Emotional Intelligence and Social Problem Solving Skills

SOCIAL PROBLEM SOLVING

> **GOAL**
>
> *To have youngsters become effective problem solvers and decision-makers.*

▶ Overview

In this chapter, you will be introduced to the Interactive Course in Social Problem Solving. This software application was developed using an authoring tool called **iBuild**, which is an easy-to-use software application that was designed for use by educators who may not have a formal background in programming. Using this full-featured, multi-media authoring tool, it was possible to create an interactive program that highlights some of the key principles of emotional intelligence. The program can be used both independently by children, once they are introduced to the concepts of emotional intelligence, and, by an adult, to delve further into the content that is included within the program. The program is highly interactive and uses a combination of text, sound, animation, and graphics to create an inviting environment for youngsters to explore the various facets of emotional intelligence. This program was intended to be both exploratory and interactive, so it does not need to be done sequentially.

▶ Time Frame for the Activity

Clinicians should plan on working on this activity over a minimum three- to four-session time frame. There are several components to this activity: a simple relaxation technique, communication skills, and a mnemonic to help in the area of social decision making.

▶ Clinical Rationale

It is becoming increasingly challenging for youngsters to develop their emotional intelligence. Some leading psychologists have commented that children today are growing up in environments that lead too many of them to lack the skills of emotional literacy:

- **being aware of one's own feelings and those of others**
- **showing empathy and understanding others' points of view**

- regulating and coping positively with emotional and behavioral impulses
- being positive goal and plan oriented
- using effective social skills in handling relationships

With these goals in mind, this chapter highlights some innovative ways to tackle the problem of helping children to achieve these important skills. In this chapter, we share some commercially available software, which was developed by the authors, to address the areas of emotional intelligence and social problem solving and decision making.

▶ *Developmental Considerations*

Many youngsters in the age group of 8–10 are still not proficient at typing and may need to use the therapist for the typing of text. Also, some of the children in this category may have perceptual motor difficulties or learning disabilities and may have difficulty with reading the text on the screen. The therapist should keep in mind that the Interactive Course in Social Problem Solving was developed for elementary-aged children and takes into account both reading and learning disabilities. The computer can speak many of the text items on the Interactive Course in Social Problem Solving.

MINIMUM MATERIALS	OPTIONAL MATERIALS	THERAPEUTIC APPLICATIONS
Interactive Course in Social Problem Solving, available for Macintosh,	printer	peer conflicts, family conflicts, depression, school problems, parent-child conflicts, and issues surrounding authority

▶ *What to Prepare in Advance*

The therapist will need to have a copy of the program, Interactive Course in Social Problem Solving, installed on a computer and be familiar with it before using it with the child.

GETTING STARTED

1 Open up the Interactive Course in Social Problem Solving by double clicking on the icon.

SPS

2 The opening screen will be displayed on the computer screen.

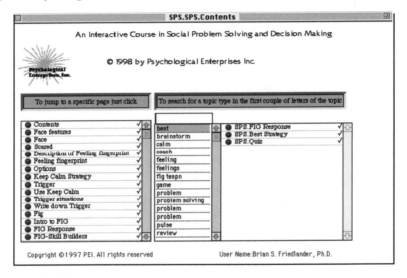

Opening Screen

3 Select a topic of interest by clicking on the list, which is on the left part of the screen. For example, to begin to teach youngsters about how to identify the signs of different feelings in themselves click on the topic "Faces." This brings up a rather playful screen that allows children to manipulate the features on a face by clicking on them. Young children will enjoy the opportunity to change the features. This activity begins to sensitize youngsters to how others may be feeling based on the facial expression. Use this as an opportunity to help children develop and increase their feelings vocabulary.

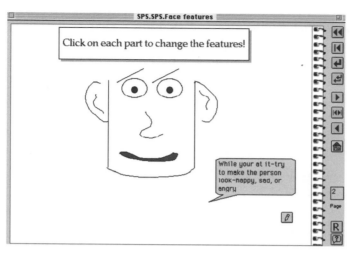

Facial Features

❹ As the therapist, once you have sensitized the children to look at the facial features of others, then you can show them real pictures of youngsters in various emotional states and find out just how good they are at figuring out how they are feeling.

❺ Click on the home page icon to take you to the opening screen. Then, scroll down and click on the lesson called Feelings Vocabulary from the list presented on the left-hand side of the page. This will bring up the following screen:

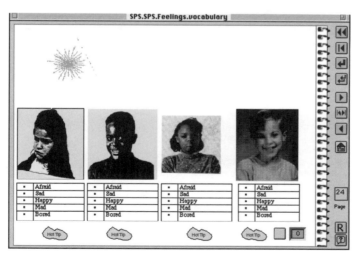

Feelings Vocabulary

6 In this activity, the children will be able to view real-life pictures of children and try to determine how they are feeling based on their facial features and body language. This is a great opportunity to talk with the children about body language and how it conveys meaning in the context of social interactions. The children you are working with are then prompted by the computer to figure out how the children are feeling and given hints, if they need them, to complete the task. In this game-like manner, children are learning the invaluable skill of looking for signs of different feelings in others.

7 One of the cardinal tenets of emotional intelligence is the necessity of children to become aware of their own feelings. This is handled in a unique way in this program by using the metaphor of a feeling fingerprint. The therapist discusses with the child that everyone has a fingerprint, and each one is unique. In a similar vein, while all children have feelings, they are all unique and expressed and experienced differently. This is especially true when we are feeling stressed. With this as a backdrop, the program takes the child through a series of screens explaining the concept and has the child begin to identify his or her unique feelings fingerprint. (For adolescents, we sometimes use the term, "stress signatures," to help make the same point.)

8 Go back to the home page by clicking on the home page icon ⌂ and then scroll down and click on the lesson called "Description of Feeling Fingerprint" from the list presented on the left-hand side of the page.

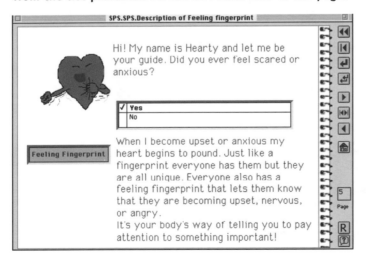

Description of Feeling Fingerprint

9 After the description of the feeling fingerprint is presented, have the child click on the next screen button ▶ to bring up the following screen.

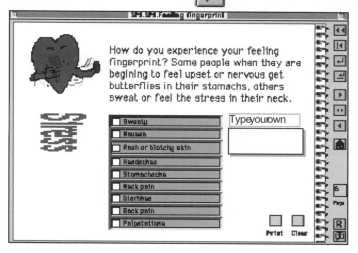

Feeling Fingerprint

Here, children can begin to think about the various ways their bodies let them know that they are under stress. The therapist can use this as a jumping off point to discuss this concept and expand upon the partial list that was included in the program.

10 Have the child click on various ways their bodies let them know that they are under stress. If the child would like, there is also room for them to type in a feeling fingerprint that was not included on the list. When the child has completed this activity, click on the Print button, and the child will then have a record that he/she can go back and refer to at home.

11 Now that the child has identified their feeling fingerprint, and we have given him or her a way to label strong feelings, it is time to talk about what options children have when they have a difficult time managing such strong impulses and feelings.

⑫ **Click on the Next Page button and bring up the Keep Calm Strategy. One of the hallmarks of the emotionally intelligent youngster is the capability to regulate and cope positively with emotions and impulses.**

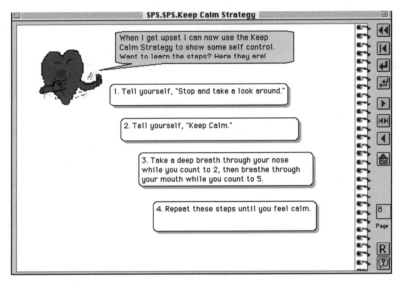

Keep Calm Strategy

The children will learn a simple, but effective, relaxation exercise to use when they are experiencing strong emotions, regardless of where they are. We have found that the Keep Calm Strategy works best when adults in the environment prompt the child to use it at appropriate times. You may also want to brainstorm some other ways that the child could relax in the face of strong feelings.

⑬ **Interacting effectively with others is difficult for some children. Teaching children how to use positive, effective social skills is often one of the most important areas to work on. We have included a strategy called BEST, which is a mini-assertiveness training program. The BEST strategy is made up of four simple steps, which are manageable for them to remember. It is important to tell the them that this takes a long time to learn and requires a lot of practice. As they remember these four, simple steps, they become more skillful in their social interactions and are more readily accepted by their peers. Have the child click on the BEST strategy lesson to learn about the skills.**

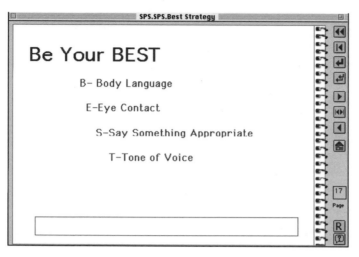

Best Strategy

After the child has learned the steps, and the therapist has modeled it, it is necessary for the child and the therapist to role-play. Children will find this activity fun. It is helpful if the therapist makes mistakes and doesn't use the BEST steps effectively so that the child can identify where the therapist has gone wrong. Be sure to exaggerate how a monster and a mouse would look if they acted out the BEST skills. You will find that the children you work with will be more critical than one would imagine. But for this activity, we are sensitizing them to the skills. If the adults in the child's world are also aware of the strategy, they can prompt them with "Be your BEST." Parents and teachers find it easy to learn and use the prompt once you have presented it to a child.

⑭ One of the last skills to be mastered by the children we work with is learning how to make appropriate social decisions. Too often, children are impulsive and have a real difficult time envisioning the consequences of their actions. By the time they have thought about something they have already done it, and it has led to generally negative ramifications. The Interactive Course in Social Problem Solving includes several screens, which introduce FIG TESPN. FIG TESPN is an acronym for a social problem solving strategy, which is helpful when talking about decision making for children. Children benefit from being able to give the strategy this unique name. FIG can be thought of as a coach who stands on the sidelines while the child makes the on-field decisions. Click on the lesson called an Introduction to FIG to get started.

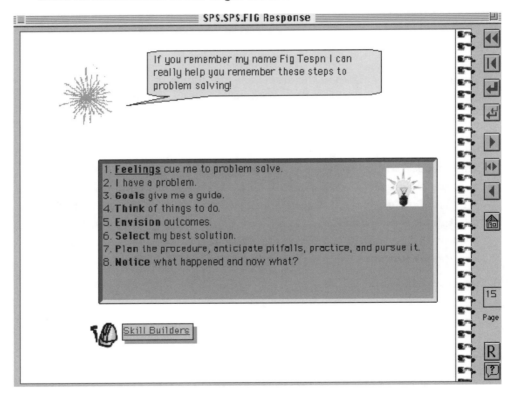

FIG TESPN Strategy

Children enjoy envisioning for themselves what FIG TESPN looks like. Here is an opportunity to use the creative skills of the children and have them draw a picture or use the computer to bring FIG TESPN to life.

While the Interactive Course in Social Problem Solving is a great way to teach elementary school-aged children the foundation skills they will need to become good social problem solvers and decision makers, it is just the first part of the equation. It is now time to introduce another software program, which was developed by the authors, to help guide children and adolescents towards making good social decisions.

As children enter early adolescence, the middle-school years, and then high school, they find themselves confronted by peer pressure and many choices to be made. Based on FIG TESPN, we have created software to guide middle- and high-school youngsters through the steps necessary to clarify their thoughts and feelings and arrive at responsible and effective actions to reach their goals. The software is engaging because it is not didactic. Rather, it starts and ends with the troublesome situations, problems, and choices children bring to it. Hence, it is called the Personal Problem Solving Guide.

Using the Personal Problem Solving Guide

THE PROBLEM SOLVING GUIDE

GOAL

*To have children become effective problem solvers
and decision-makers.*

▶ Overview

The Personal Problem Solving Guide is for those who work with middle- and high-school-aged children. At some time, most children experience discipline problems, personal problems, emotional problems, academic difficulties, family problems, problems with teachers, or other personal or interpersonal issues. The Personal Problem Solving Guide provides a means for assisting children's problem solving and decision making. The Personal Problem Solving Guide gives the youngster the opportunity to work through a personal problem, using a non-threatening software application.

The Personal Problem Solving Guide brings ideas, events, feelings, and ideas into new relationships. This allows children to approach problems in ways that they had not seen before. The computer format helps connect thinking with behavior. This releases children, and those who work with them, from emotional logjams that jumble feelings, stifle thinking, and disrupt positive, goal-directed behaviors.

The Personal Problem Solving Guide can be used in detention, discipline situations, counseling sessions, and for dispute and conflict resolution. It can be used any time there is a problem that children need to think through. This Guide can be used to teach prevention skills to high-risk youth, either as an adjunct to an existing prevention program or by itself. This program has also been used to teach conflict resolution to peer mediators. It is designed to be used by members of child study teams, school-based support teams, school resource committees, pupil assistance teams, guidance counselors, disciplinarians, assistant/vice principals, teachers, school nurses, clinicians, and those working in centers dealing with children's learning problems. There are two versions of the Personal Problem Solving Guide included in this program. The first is entered by the keyword,

PROBLEM, and is used when children have a problem, issue, or decision to think about. The second is entered by the keyword, TROUBLE, and is used when children have gotten into detention or other discipline-related or academic difficulty and need to think through what happened and how they can resolve it or avoid the same trouble in the future. Both versions yield an action plan that youngsters can use to implement their ideas. See the figure on the following page to view the actual computer screen.

▶ *Time Frame for the Activity*

Initially, clinicians should plan on working on this activity over a two-session time frame to train the child and run through an issue. Similarly, the therapist can use this software application at any time when the child needs to think through a problematic situation.

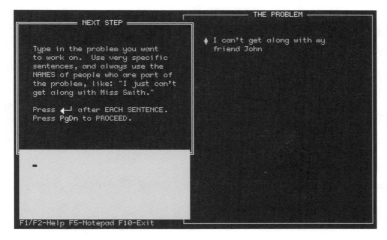

Screen Showing Student Identifying their Problem

▶ *Clinical Rationale*

The Personal Problem Solving Guide can be used with both middle-school and high-school age children. Younger children may be able to access the program with help and assistance from an adult, especially when they have to read the directions on the screen (the text is written at a third-grade reading level).

Some children experience problems that are of an internalizing nature, that is, they seem to be the main individuals suffering because of their problems, and they tend to keep their feelings and thoughts pretty much to themselves. They may tend to anticipate failure and futility, and, therefore, be resistant to even trying something new. It is important to take special steps to motivate them to use the Personal Problem Solving Guide. With these individuals, it may be helpful to take a laid-back but supportive approach. It is often helpful to reflect their feelings of sadness or futility. Supportive encouragement and walking them through the Personal Problem Solving Guide in a spirit of exploration can lessen their anxiety to some degree. As they get involved in the program, they often feel empowered. In addition, because they are interacting with a computer rather than a person, they usually do not display the hesitation or resistance associated with anticipation of ridicule and rejection by others.

It is important not to be critical as you work with them. Even if they make a mistake in one of the steps, try to avoid correcting them initially. Let the logical consequences of their thinking unfold as they continue to work through the process. As a mistake becomes obvious, impedes further problem solving, or looks like it might lead to a harmful outcome, feign confusion ("I'm not sure I followed everything up to this point. Let's just run back through this again so I can understand it.") and, with the child, go back (Page Up) to review areas where the response, and the thinking, need to be reconsidered.

Others tend more towards externalizing and aggressiveness. When they are in a hostile, angry, or blaming frame of mind, they are not especially receptive to positive approaches to problem solving. With these children, it is important to focus on the Personal Problem Solving Guide as a means of helping them get what they want. For example, if they think that all of their friends are against them, or that some teachers have a grudge against them and treat them unfairly, do not dispute this. Rather, use the problem as they see it. For example, this would mean dealing with the problem of how to get their friends to not be against them, or to keep the teachers from expressing grudges against them. Of course, inherent in this is getting them to realize what they really want, such as graduating from the grade they are in, not getting detentions, and having friends. It may be necessary to be especially patient and non-confrontational when first working on the Personal Problem Solving Guide. Do not be surprised by an initial lack of seriousness. However, express your confidence that this is not beyond them, and that "youngsters your age usually can give at least a couple of answers" for each step. The reason for doing this is that, after they exhaust inappropriate responses, they will begin to include some more appropriate ones. Then, you can focus on these responses and still be working constructively and within the their frame of reference.

▶ *Developmental Considerations*

Middle- and high-school-aged youngsters will benefit by using the Personal Problem Solving Guide to sort out their difficulties. Those with learning disabilities may need the therapist to read the screen directions on the Personal Problem Solving Guide. Likewise, some of them may need assistance in how they organize their ideas. But bear in mind, as long as the child can understand what they have written, it is not important to be concerned about spelling.

MINIMUM MATERIALS	OPTIONAL MATERIALS	THERAPEUTIC APPLICATIONS
Personal Problem Solving Guide available for computers running Windows	printer	peer conflicts, family conflicts, school problems, decision-making

▶ *What to Prepare in Advance*

The program can either be installed on the hard drive or run from the disk. The set up for using the Personal Problem Solving Guide requires an IBM-compatible computer, with a 3.5-inch disk drive. A printer is recommended so they can take a printed copy of the action plan home. For Macintosh users, the program also can be used by combining SoftPC, SoftWindows, or Virtual PC. As long as you have access to a computer that can run MS-DOS, the program will operate effectively. For ease and independence of use, the program has been designed with a minimal number of commands that need to be performed. These are displayed clearly on the screen. Further context-sensitive help is built into the program and is always accessible by using the function keys on the keyboard.

▶ *Preparing the Child*

When presenting the Personal Problem Solving Guide to youngsters, you want to be sure that they view it as a tool to help them meet goals that they care about. They have to buy into it so that they will take it seriously and use it productively. If it is presented as "work" or as "punishment," the value of the activity will be diminished and there will be little likelihood that they will carry out their action plan.

▶ *Getting Started*

The Personal Problem Solving Guide moves the youngster through different stages during the session. During Stage I, the program begins with a child typing his or her name and grade level for identification. This information is captured so that it is affixed to the action plan once it is printed out.

During Stage II, children are asked to identify what happened to get them into trouble or the context of the problem and are instructed to be as specific as possible when typing in their responses. Stage II presents a context for the decision making and problem solving to commence and sensitizes the youngster to look for signs of different feelings, an important skill in the decision-making process.

Stage III is designed to help them consider the problem in a few different ways, and allows them to begin to think of some things they could do about it. For this stage in the process, the computer program has been designed with an algorithm, which brings back text that has already been typed into the program by the youngster into a new prompt that moves the problems-solving process ahead. For example, youngsters are asked to list every way they can think of to accomplish the goal that they mentioned during Stage II of the process. The software automatically brings forward each goal the youngster typed into the program during Stage II and allows them to respond to it. In this way, they begin to develop a list of possible alternative behaviors. Additionally, the program has been developed to bring up youngsters' responses during Stage II and prompt them to formulate what they can do to keep the behavior from happening again.

During Stage IV, they are able to select from the screen a list of alternative actions that they generated during the computer session. The software automatically compiles the list in a way that can be easily reviewed and prioritized. The graphic below is an example of the computer screen and displays an alternative behavior that has been marked a realistic strategy to help reach a the goal.

NEXT STEP	ACTIONS BEING SELECTED
Take a good look at ALL your ideas at the right. Select the ONE that you feel is the BEST. Then select another good one, and another. Only choose a few that you REALLY WANT TO TRY.	1. I could have gotten involved in the discussion I could have apologized ♦ Talk about this problem Stay awake

Simulated Personal Problem Solving Guide Screen Showing
Action Selected should be marked in (♦) Among Alternatives

In the final stage, children are guided through a detailed look at their choices and are given the chance to do some planning about what it will take for their ideas to be carried out realistically and in the face of possible obstacles or "roadblocks."

▶ *How to run the Personal Problem Solving Guide*

To use the Personal Problem Solving Guide program, insert the disk into your disk drive. If the disk is in the "A" drive, get to the A:\> prompt in DOS and type "Winsight", or in the "B" drive, get to the B:\> prompt in DOS and type

"Winsight". After typing "Winsight" press the Enter key. The program will prompt you to enter either one of the two versions of the Personal Problem Solving Guide, which are on the disk. The first is entered by typing the keyword, PROBLEM, and is used when children have a problem, issue, or decision that they are thinking about. The second is entered by typing the keyword, TROUBLE, and is used when children have gotten into detention, or other discipline-related or academic difficulty, and need to think through what happened.

If you are using an emulation program on the Macintosh (i.e. VirtualPC or SoftWindows), follow these steps. Open the emulation from your hard disk. When you see the C: prompt, type B: and hit the Return key. Now type "Winsight" and hit the Return key. Set the Number Lock to Off by selecting Command-N. Proceed as above by typing in the keyword PROBLEM or TROUBLE. If you do not have an extended keyboard, you can Page Up by using the Command-U sequence and Page Down by using the Command-W sequence. To take advantage of the function keys on the Macintosh, use the Command key followed by the appropriate number. For example, to emulate the F9 function key, hold down the Command key, and then press the 9 key.

▶ *Turning Action Plans into Success*

The Personal Problem Solving Guide generates two types of printouts. The first is a Plan of Action. The second is a Context Outline. Each has its own use.

The Action Plan gives individuals a list of things that they can do to solve the problem or prevent trouble in the future. This plan is based on the ideas that they have generated with the Personal Problem Solving Guide. Because it contains the children's own ideas, it is more likely that they will implement them. In addition, the plan can be made more detailed and complex through a part of the program that helps the child anticipate and address obstacles.

It is important for the adult to review the Action Plan prior to it being implemented. Some individuals may be unrealistic about what they will be able to do and would, therefore, benefit from thinking through the plan a little more. The adult may also wish to raise a few obstacles unanticipated by youngsters. The purpose here is not for the adult to take over the problem solving process, but to facilitate youngsters' further thinking and planning. They will respond to this deepening because it reveals to them ideas that were "in them" that they did not realize. Also, children can learn a great deal from seeing some relatively ineffective problem solving on their part, and the benefits of rethinking and engaging in the problem solving process often.

Once the plan is finalized, the adult can then help it take shape by asking who, what, when, where, and how. In other words:

- **"Who will do this?" "Who else needs to be involved?"**
- **"What will you do?" "What will you say?"**
- **"What else could you say?" "What do you think he will say?"**
- **"When are you going to do this?" "When are you going to do the next step?" "When are you going to do the other things?"**
- **"Where will you do this?" "Where else could you do this?"**

The key phase of putting the plan into action, the "how" involves role-playing. There is no doubt that the more concrete and realistic a learning experience is for them, the more likely they are to carry that learning into the real world and their everyday experiences. Have youngsters act out exactly how they would implement the plan, what they would say, how they would say it, etc. An adult can play the other role(s) and react as a real person might react. Through this role-play, certain skill deficits may be noted and targeted for future work. For example, if a child is going to talk to another and you notice unassertive posture, a lack of eye contact, and an unsteady tone of voice, it may be necessary to work on these areas prior to their implementing a plan (see BEST discussed earlier).

Once the child has a reasonable action plan and has practiced some of the necessary skills to implement it, the plan can serve as an informal contract. The contract can be between an adult and youngster or even a contract with the child and himself or herself. Inherent in a contract is the sense of social obligation, as well as a means of monitoring that the obligation has been met. It is important that adults follow up on the action plan, to see if and how it was implemented and also what the results were. This follow up can occur through discussion at a preset future meeting, or, by youngsters writing the results of their actions on the print out of the action plan.

After implementation of an action plan, it may be necessary for youngsters to go back to the plan and come up with more ideas. Or, youngsters may have additional problems to resolve, which require going back to the Personal Problem Solving Guide. Regardless of whether they have been successful or whether they have to go back to the drawing board, they should be reinforced for thinking through the problem and taking action on it.

▶ *Ending a Session on the Computer*

The computer problem solving session can end in several ways. If the child has gone through all the stages, he or she could print out a copy of their Action Plan, which would list all of the things they are going to do to solve their problem. If a child was unable to complete the session, perhaps due to lack of time, it can be saved to his/her own problem solving diskette or file and worked on at another time. Under appropriate circumstances, a diskette can even be taken home to continue the problem solving process.

The Context Outline is a detailed, printed analysis of the session, including all prompts and responses to them. This can be valuable as a full record of the meeting with the child. This provides essential documentation, which can be entered into relevant records. It also provides a tangible written record, which can be shared with others, as is appropriate.

CLINICAL CASE ILLUSTRATION

Barry is a seventh-grade student who has been diagnosed as having attention-deficit hyperactivity disorder. He has had both academic and social difficulties in the past. Barry was recently referred to the school psychologist for being disruptive in class and for talking back to his teachers. The principal, who had referred Barry to the school psychologist, was concerned because, while in the past, Barry might call out in class and be impulsive, this was the first incident where he became quite defiant towards the teacher and disrupted the class session. The principal was also concerned when he spoke with Barry about the incident that he did not see the seriousness of what he had done despite the fact that he was suspended from school for two days.

Barry met with the school psychologist upon his reentry to the school, along with his parents and the principal. The school psychologist recommended that he begin to work with Barry and try to help him find alternative ways to deal with his frustration and behavioral outbursts. Barry was initially hesitant to revisit the incident and just shrugged it off to his impulsiveness. The school psychologist could see that Barry was upset about something, and that it was going to take some time before Barry was going to be willing to talk about it. The school psychologist decided to use the Personal Problem Solving Guide to reach Barry in a non-confrontational, engaging manner. The school psychologist ventured that Barry may be more willing to work through his problem using the computer, rather than initially wanting to talk about it. As Barry worked through the Personal Problem Solving Guide, he was encouraged to look at his behavior and come up with alternative solutions when presented with a similar problem. While Barry would have a tendency to want to rush through the process and jump from screen to screen, with the guidance from the school psychologist, Barry would be willing to reflect on his responses and think a little more about the prompts that were on the screen. At times, the school psychologist engaged Barry in a general discussion about the topic on the computer screen or self-disclosed how he might react to such a

CLINICAL CASE ILLUSTRATION

situation in order to stimulate Barry's thinking. Interestingly, Barry was not resistant to stopping and taking more time. Personal Problem Solving Guide users have found that special needs students are willing to interface longer and more often with a computer than with a person. As Barry interacted with the school psychologist and worked through his problem using the Personal Problem Solving Guide, he began to understand that there were other ways of seeing and coping with his problem.

Users of the Personal Problem Solving Guide have found that it is an invaluable tool to help diagnose where youngsters get stuck in the social problem solving process. With this in mind, the school psychologist noted during one of their sessions that Barry was unable to think of alternative solutions to problem situations. The Personal Problem Solving Guide gave the school psychologist a window into the problem, which was very real for Barry. While Barry could identify the problem area and identify his feelings, he was extremely deficient in his ability to brainstorm and come up with creative or new solutions to his problem. With this information, the school psychologist began to dialogue with Barry and helped him to see that there may be additional alternatives to help solve his problem.

A copy of the action plan is included, which summarizes the sessions that Barry had with the school psychologist. Working with Barry, it became clear that he had responded well to using the Personal Problem Solving Guide to help resolve his problem. In subsequent sessions with Barry, the school psychologist spent more time looking at what obstacles he might encounter as he went out to try to put his action plan into effect. The Personal Problem Solving Guide gave the school psychologist another tool that engaged the youngster and opened up the dialogue for successful problem solving.

CLINICAL CASE ILLUSTRATION

Sample Output of Action Plan

The Personal Problem Solving Guide

© 1992 Winsight Inc.

Date: 9/19/98   Time: 10:04:52 AM

YOUR NAME:
— Barry

YOUR GRADE & TEACHER:
— 7

THE PROBLEM:
— calling out in class

— yelling at the teachers

FEELINGS I GET:
— when I am in Mr. Smith's class I feel stupid

— sometimes, I feel really angry

WHAT I CAN DO:
1. I could talk to Mr. Smith about getting extra help.

2. I could speak to my school psychologist.

3. I could speak to my friends about the problem.

NOTE PAD:
— This is a good idea.

— Try it next time.

This Action Plan was made on 9/19/98
with the Personal Problem Solving Guide.

Ways to Access the Computer for Students with Special Needs

STUDENTS WITH SPECIAL NEEDS

> ### GOAL
>
> *To ensure computer access for children with special needs.*

▶ Overview

Many of the activities outlined in this book are intrinsically motivating and allow clinicians to work with children in an engaging manner. These activities allow clinicians to build rapport and more efficiently help children find solutions to their difficulties. One of the problems that may be encountered by clinicians is a child's inability to adequately access the computer. Many children with learning and social/emotional disabilities may have difficulty using a mouse, constructing sentences, or using the keyboard effectively. In this chapter we will outline some strategies and approaches that can be used to give children more effective access to the computer.

▶ Overcoming Keyboard Troubles

One of the primary ways to enter text into the computer is via the keyboard. For many children with fine motor difficulties, the keyboard often gets in the way of their being able to use the aforementioned software applications. For some children, the keys on the standard keyboard are just too small and do not provide an adequate target for them. To address this concern, there are a number of companies that manufacture alternative keyboards with large keys and large letters on each of the keys. Young children who are just learning the alphabet, or who may have visual or perceptual difficulties, really enjoy working on a keyboard with large keys and with the letters prominently displayed.

The Big Keys Keyboard looks very much like a standard keyboard, except for the fact that the keys are much larger and the letters are prominently displayed on each of the keys. Likewise, there is the option of purchasing the Big Keys keyboard with the letters in alphabetical order, which helps some children navigate around the keyboard with more confidence and comfort. The Big Keys Keyboard is available for both Windows and Macintosh compatible computers. These keyboards are easily attached to the computer via a cable and will replace the standard keyboard when using it with students.

Big Keys

If you have experimented with the use of the Big Keys Keyboard and still find that some of the children you work with are still having difficulty getting around the keyboard, you may want to take a look at the Intellikeys keyboard. The Intellikeys keyboard is often characterized as a programmable keyboard. Programmable keyboards let the clinician create what are called overlays to slide into the Intellikeys keyboard. The Intellikeys keyboard comes with six standard overlays that includes the QWERTY layout and various alphabetical layouts. Sliding any of the six standard overlays into the Intellikeys programs the keyboard to accept the letter or number that is on each of the keys.

Intellikeys Keyboard with Overlay

One of the advantages of the Intellikeys keyboard is the ability to set certain keyboard parameters, which customizes the experience for the children. If you were working with children with motor difficulties, you would be able to set the amount of time the children would need to press a key before the computer accepted the letter. Similarly, the clinician could turn off the repeat key feature so that no matter how long a key was pressed it would only register as one letter. One of the nice features of the Intellikeys keyboard is the ability to have someone create customized overlays that meet youngsters' individual needs, using an accompanying program called Overlay Maker.

For some children with motor issues, it may be advisable to look at using what are called on-screen keyboards. Just as the name suggests, these keyboards actually float on your monitor screen and can be accessed using a mouse, trackball, or a joystick. When the on-screen keyboard appears, the child can simply type by using the mouse and clicking on the desired letter, one at a time. Since the on-screen keyboards are merely software, it often ships with several different sized on-screen keyboards. This gives the clinician the ability to quickly change the size of the keyboard based on the need of the child. Many children who have well-developed mouse skills will find it rather easy to adjust to using an on-screen keyboard.

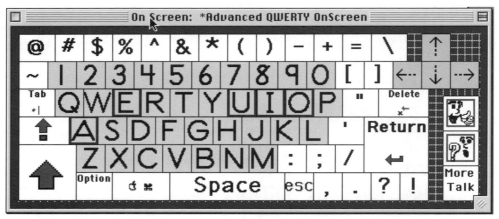

Discover: Screen: On-Screen Keyboard

▶ *Writing Aids*

One of the areas that children with learning disabilities often complain the most about is writing. Children with learning disabilities often have a hard time organizing their thoughts, sequencing their ideas, and coming up with topics or themes to write about. When they finally have figured out what to write about, they are usually hesitant to express themselves for fear of misspelling a word. Many children with writing difficulties usually write using three to four letter words and simple sentences and paragraphs, and are afraid to venture from this path. One of the writing tools that are helpful to use at the beginning of the writing process is a program called Inspiration.

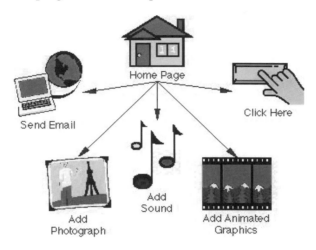

Inspiration Web

Inspiration is an ideal tool when children are brainstorming writing ideas. It is a graphical outlining and brainstorming tool that allows children to begin the writing process by creating a webbing, using graphics. Once the clinician and child have created the graphical web, with a click of the mouse, the program will create a standard outline they can use for their written work. Having both a text, as well as a graphical outline, allows children the freedom to express their ideas in different ways.

Of all the software applications that support the writing process, the most indispensable is Word Prediction Software. Word Prediction Software was first introduced to help eliminate the number of keystrokes needed to type a sentence. For this reason, it is a wonderful tool for children with learning and/or attentional problems. Word Prediction Software uses algorithms to predict the word that you are thinking of using on the basis of frequency, grammatical usage, and recency of use. Words that are frequently used in the English language are assigned a higher frequency count and are predicted more often than words with a lower assigned frequency count. When frequency and grammar are both considered it makes it easier for children to construct well-formed sentences. More importantly, children can express themselves using more complex sentences and words to relate their ideas.

Here is an example. One of the leading word prediction programs in the K–12 marketplace is Co:Writer 4000. Co:Writer 4000 works with just about any word processor to help predict words. As the writer begins to type words into the sentence, Co:Writer 4000 begins predicting which word the writer wanted to use. For example, if you wanted to use the word "yesterday," you would begin to type the word out, and by the time you typed "yes," you would see that the word, "yesterday," has popped up in a predicted list of possible words. To use that word in the sentence, you could select it with the mouse, or press the number assigned to the word in the list. After you have created your sentence and inserted an ending punctuation mark, the sentence is transferred to your word processor.

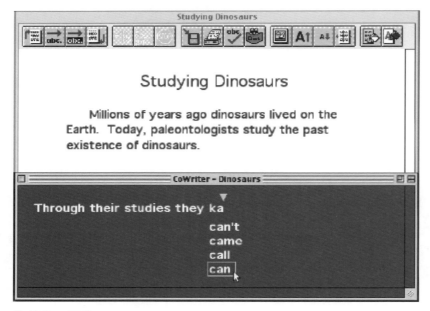

Co:Writer 4000

In addition to the word prediction capability, Co:Writer 4000 has a feature called FlexSpell, which anticipates the errors that writers make when misspelling certain words. This allows for efficient correction. Overall, Co:Writer 4000 works in unison with word processors and allows children to both craft their ideas with less effort and eliminates a large number of keystrokes. Another exciting thing about Co:Writer 4000 is its ability to link to other applications besides just word processors. Co:Writer 4000 links up to many multimedia programs, such as PowerPoint and Hyperstudio, so children can enjoy the benefits of word prediction within these highly interactive applications. Co:Writer 4000 simply needs to be linked to an application that has a text box, and then it will be able to predict words into that application. Children, therefore, can become actively involved in the activity and not be as concerned with spelling and typing.

▶ *Talking Word Processors*

Some children with learning and attentional problems may benefit from some of the talking word processors now available. A number of studies have found that children who used talking word processors did a better job of being able to proofread the material that they wrote. One of the more popular talking word processors is Write Outloud.

Write Outloud

Write Outloud is a user friendly talking word processor that allows the user to copy, paste, and insert pictures into the word processing document. It is not nearly as powerful as Microsoft Word, but it does perform an excellent job when it comes to reading text that is typed into the document. Likewise, the program includes the Talking Franklin Spell Checker, which picks up on homonym errors and the kind of spelling errors children with learning disabilities tend to make. Other advantages to this program are its ease of use and the clean interface. Once you get it up and running, you will quickly find out just how easy it is to use. The program comes with a library of clip art pictures that can be inserted into word processing documents. Write Outloud also allows the user the capability to customize the working environment by changing the color of the background and the color of the text. This is consistent with findings of researchers in the field of special education that suggest that some children with learning and attentional problems respond positively to different color combinations of the background and of the text. If you are working with children who could benefit from the auditory feedback, then this program is an excellent addition to your tool kit and can be used in place of Microsoft Word for the activities mentioned in this book. This program is available for both Windows and Macintosh computers.

One the newest and most unique talking word processors to be released is called Intellitalk II. What sets Intellitalk II apart from other talking word processors is the capability to create what Intellikeys has termed palettes or word/picture banks. These palettes can be displayed on the screen and can contain text and pictures. The palettes can then be positioned on the top, bottom right, and left of the screen. When the user clicks on one of the items in a palette, it can be set up so that the item speaks. Then, Intellitalk II will insert the text that has been set up with the item on the screen.

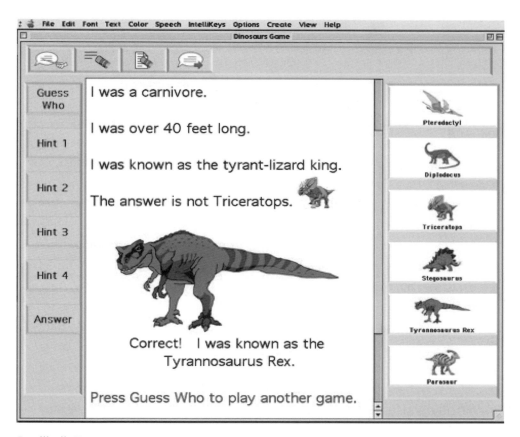

Intellitalk II

The combinations of how this can be used are endless. The clinician can also set up Intellitalk II to display the picture and the accompanying text when an item from the palette is selected. Think of this tool as a way to set up both picture and word banks that children can access without the need to know how to type. The clinician could easily set up both a word and a picture bank that children could then use to express their feelings and write their stories.

Using this program would relieve some children from having to type. Additionally, it is possible to create the equivalent of an on-screen keyboard so that students who are not touch typists could simply click on a palette item to spell words. For those children with significant motor involvement, it is possible to set use of the palettes with the Intellikeys keyboard with a single switch, thereby giving children with motor issues the capability of participating in these clinical activities. Generally, children are able to take advantage of their visual or picture vocabularies without being limited by their motor capabilities.

CLINICAL CASE ILLUSTRATION

James was a ten-year-old youngster who recently moved into the district from out of state. He was in a regular fifth grade classroom in the upper elementary school. Based on his previous records, it appeared that James had very good verbal skills. After two months of school being in session, his teacher, Mrs. Smith referred James for a consultation by the child study team. Mrs. Smith was concerned that, while James seemed bright enough, he was not getting his work done and he was having difficulty making friends and interacting with the other students in the classroom. Mrs. Smith had observed that James had a hard time staying on task and needed a great deal of teacher monitoring in order to accomplish his work. James was also very unorganized, and he had a hard time keeping his papers and assignments in an organized fashion. While the other students tolerated him, James had no friends in the classroom and was not adept in the social arena. James was subsequently referred to the child study team and was evaluated by the school psychologist and learning consultant.

On the basis of the psychologist's evaluation, James was also seen by a child psychiatrist to help with a differential diagnosis and to plan his educational program. While James had strong cognitive skills, his behavior and social deficits clearly set him apart from his peers, and he was eventually diagnosed with Asperger Syndrome. The psychologist noted in his report that James had a very difficult time understanding his feelings and the feelings of his classmates. His social skills were weak, and he often had a hard time picking up on the non-verbal, social cues in his environment.

The therapist who started to work with James decided to address his understanding of feelings, since this is an area that is decidedly weak in many children with Asperger Syndrome. The therapist decided to use the computer

CLINICAL CASE ILLUSTRATION

to try to address these very important life skills. The therapist initially used some pictures of children experiencing different feeling states. Since the therapist had access to Intellitalk II, she decided to use it to create a picture bank of different facial pictures. Intellitalk II was a good starting off point, since it included a picture library of clip art of both boys and girls, which depicted different emotional states. The therapist reasoned that it would be most advantageous to start out using clip art pictures before moving to more real life examples. Similarly, by using a talking word processor, the student would be more engaged in the activity and it would make it more game like.

In this example, James could use the word bank on the right of the screen to start off his sentences about how the boy was feeling in the pictures.

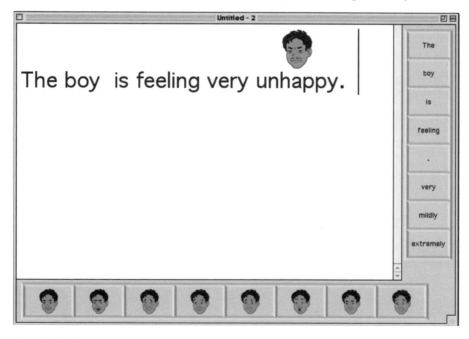

Intellitalk II

CLINICAL CASE ILLUSTRATION

Then he could click on the picture to find out how the boy was feeling. Likewise, the therapist could ask James to point out which picture exhibits the feeling of sadness, and James could simply click on the picture to see if he was right. Using the program offered the therapist opportunities to have James talk about and learn how to discern the subtleties of facial expressions. This was a fun activity and one that is a very accessible activity for the student.

Using a digital camera for this therapeutic activity added an exciting dimension to the task. In this activity, the therapist asked James to display various feeling states, which were captured with the digital camera. The therapist, for example, asked him to show a happy face, which was recorded by the digital camera. The pictures were then downloaded to the computer and added to a multimedia software package (e.g., Hyperstudio or PowerPoint) for viewing. The student got a real kick out of seeing his facial expression on the computer screen, which proved to be highly motivating. James then spent some time talking with the therapist about his different feeling states, which helped him to cue into facial features and develop his feelings vocabulary.

CLINICAL CASE ILLUSTRATION

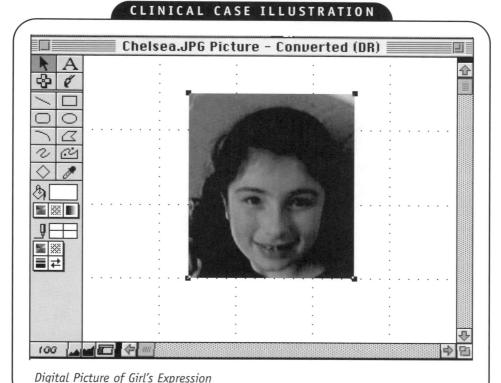

Digital Picture of Girl's Expression

ANOTHER CLINICAL CASE ILLUSTRATION

Johnny was a twelve-year-old child who had a variety of diagnoses such as Oppositional Defiant Disorder, Attention-Deficit/Hyper-activity Disorder, and learning disability before being diagnosed as having Asperger Syndrome. This diagnosis occurred late because of his good verbal skills and his ability to coexist with peers when younger, although he did not develop any close friendships. As he got older, the differences in social skills between himself and others became more pronounced. In addition, his ability to cope with change and stress in his environment deteriorated. A business trip by his parent or a substitute teacher in school was sure to set him off.

ANOTHER CLINICAL CASE ILLUSTRATION

He was doing well academically, though his handwriting skills were below par for his age group. For this reason, the clinician decided to use an on-screen keyboard. This allowed Johnny to use the mouse to type. He was usually a quiet student who enjoyed reading. However, he had no real social relationships, preferring to be alone during unstructured times. In addition, he had difficulty in unstructured and highly stimulating situations such as walking in the hall, recess, and gym class. He would occasionally become aggressive and resistant to limit-setting. Reasoning and threat of punishment had no impact on him when he was in a highly volatile state. The following social story was developed in order to help him cope proactively with stressful situations. He would read this story at home before coming to school, and occasionally during school.

Here is a brief social story that was later turned into a multimedia project with Johnny's assistance. Working on the computer project allowed the clinician and Johnny to review the steps he needed to take in school to help him cope with demands placed on him.

One of Johnny's scripts was how he was to handle himself walking in the hallway. Here is a brief synopsis of a social script that was developed with the help of the clinician.

Walking in the Hallway Script

During the day, there are times I need to walk in the hallway.

Sometimes, I walk with a few kids, and other times, I walk with my class.

There are rules of good behavior that everyone follows while walking in the hallway.

Following the rules in the hallway makes everyone happy, and gets the kids ready to do good work in the next class.

The rules are:
- no pushing
- walking quietly

ANOTHER CLINICAL CASE ILLUSTRATION

- no hitting—keep my hands to myself
- no running
- no talking back or saying rude things

If someone gets in front of me or doesn't follow the rules, it makes me feel angry. But I can't solve it by hitting or yelling. I can just remember that it happened, take a deep breath, and know that I can follow the rules.

I am responsible for my own behavior, NOT anyone else's.

Having developed the script, the clinician and Johnny set time aside to develop a multimedia project that highlighted the points in the script. The clinician envisioned that, once the multimedia project was completed, this was something that Johnny could refer to over and over again if he needed to be reminded about what he was supposed to do. Using a multimedia application like Hyperstudio, Johnny would be able to say the scripts and could also create animation to define what his hallway behavior should look like. The clinician started by using one of the ready-made cards in Hyperstudio that looks like a book. The first card would be the title card and set the stage for the project they would be working on.

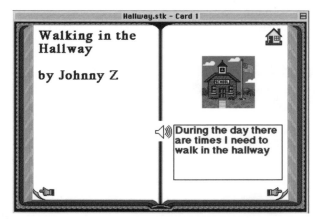

Title Card in Social Story

ANOTHER CLINICAL CASE ILLUSTRATION

The clinician then helped Johnny create a page that stated the rules for hall behavior.

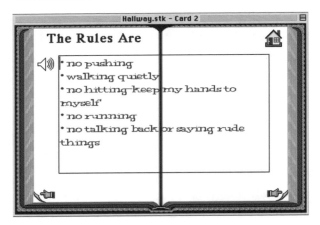

Rules for Behavior

Using the sound recording capabilities of Hyperstudio, Johnny was able to type the rules and record them into his multimedia project. Now when Johnny wanted to hear the rules, he could click on the speaker button and have the computer read them back to him. The clinician and Johnny brainstormed several things he could do when he was feeling angry and upset in the hallway and decided to put together the following card. The card shows Johnny sitting at his desk and stating that he could count to ten if he felt angry.

Things I Can Do

ANOTHER CLINICAL CASE ILLUSTRATION

The clinician then brainstormed and decided to put together a card that would highlight the reward that Johnny could receive for following his social story.

Johnny's Reward for Following His "Social Story"

As you can see, Johnny really enjoyed using the computer and wanted to be able to play a game on it with another classmate if he successfully followed his social story. Johnny was motivated to do this multimedia activity, but, more importantly, it helped reinforce the skills he needed to accomplish. He could review what he needed to do at school and at home by running through the multimedia project.

▶ *Appendix—Software Applications*

AppleWorks 5.0, ClarisWorks   Mac, PC
Apple Computer
www.apple.com

Bigkeys Keyboard
Greystone Digital, Inc.   Mac, PC
www.bigkeys.com

Hyperstudio   Mac, PC
Knowledge Adventure
www.hyperstudio.com

Hollywood High   Mac, PC
Grolier Interactive
www.gi.grolier.com

Inspiration   Mac, PC
Inspiration, Inc.
www.inspiration.com

Intellitalk II, Intellikeys Keyboard,
   Overlay Maker   Mac, PC
Intellitools, Inc
www.intellitools.com

Interactive Course in Social Problem
   Solving   Mac
Psychological Enterprises, Inc.
www.EQparenting.com

Microsoft Word, Powerpoint   Mac, PC
Microsoft
www.microsoft.com

Personal Problem Solving Guide   Mac,
   PC
Psychological Enterprises, Inc.
www.EQparenting.com

Sound Companion   Mac, PC
FTC Publishing
www.ftcpublishing.com

*i*Build   Mac
Tom Caine & Associates
www.caineassociates.com

Acrux Software
www.acruxsoft.com

Write Outloud, Co:Writer 4000,
   Discover Screen   Mac, PC
Don Johnston, Inc.
www.donjohnston.com

▶ *Supporting Print/Video Resources*

These and many other staff development resources are available from National Professional Resources, Inc. 1-800-453-7461 www.nprinc.com

Bocchino, Rob. *Emotional Literacy: To Be a Different Kind of Smart*. Thousand Oaks, CA: Corwin Press, 1999.

Elias, Maurice, Brian Friedlander, Steven Tobias. *Emotionally Intelligent Parenting: How to Raise a Self-Disciplined, Responsible, Socially Skilled Child*. New York, NY: Random House, 1999.

Elias, Maurice. *Social Decision-Making and Life Skills Development: Guidelines for Middle School Educators*. New York, NY: Three Rivers Press, 1999.

Elias, Maurice. *Raising Emotionally Intelligent Teenagers: Parenting with Love, Laughter and Limits*. New York, NY: Three Rivers Press, 1999.

Elias, Maurice, et al. *Promoting Social-Emotional Learning: Guidelines for Educators*. Alexandria, VA: ASCD, 1997.

Elias, Maurice, Brian Friedlander, Steven Tobias. *Computers in Child Therapy*. New York, NY: Three Rivers Press, 1999.

Elias, Maurice, Steven Tobias. *Social Problem Solving Interventions in the Schools*. New York, NY: Three Rivers Press, 1998.

Elias, Maurice, Steven Tobias. *Problem-Solving/Decision Making for Social and Academic Success*. New York, NY: Three Rivers Press, 1999.

Falvey, Mary A. *Inclusive and Heterogeneous Schooling: Assessment, Curriculum and Instruction*. Baltimore, MD: Paul H. Brookes Publishing, 1995.

Flick, Grad L. *ADD/ADHD Behavior-Change Resource Kit*. West Nyack, NY: Center for Applied Research in Education, 1998.

Gardner, Howard. *The Disciplined Mind: What All Students Should Understand*. New York, NY: Simon & Schuster, 1999.

Gardner, Howard. *How Are Kids Smart?* (Video) Port Chester, NY: National Professional Resources, Inc., 1996.

Glasser William. *Alternative Strategies to Social Promotion* (Video). Port Chester, NY: National Professional Resources, Inc., 1998.

Goleman, Daniel. *Emotional Intelligence: Why It Can Matter More Than I.Q.* New York, NY: Bantam Books, 1995.

Goleman, Daniel. *Emotional Intelligence: A New Vision for Educators* (Video). Port Chester, NY: National Professional Resources, Inc., 1996.

Harwell, Joan M. *Ready-To-Use Information & Materials for Assessing Specific Learning Disabilities, Volume I.* West Nyack, NY: Center for Applied Research in Education, 1995.

Harwell, Joan M. *Ready-To-Use Tools & Materials for Remediating Specific Learning Disabilities, Volume II.* West Nyack, NY: Center for Applied Research in Education, 1993.

Janney, Rachel, Martha E. Snell. *Behavioral Support.* Baltimore, MD: Paul H. Brookes Publishing, 2000.

Janney, Rachel, Martha E. Snell. *Modifying Schoolwork.* Baltimore, MD: Paul H. Brookes Publishing, 2000.

Jensen, Eric. *The Fragile Brain: What Impairs Learning and What We Can Do About It.* (Video) Port Chester, NY: National Professional Resources, Inc., 2000.

Jensen, Eric. *Practical Applications of Brain-Based Learning.* (Video) Port Chester, NY: National Professional Resources, Inc., 2000.

Kerzner-Lipsky, Dorothy, & Alan Gartner. *Standards & Inclusion: Can We Have Both?* (Video). Port Chester, NY: National Professional Resources, Inc., 1998.

Kerzner-Lipsky, Dorothy & Alan Gartner. *Inclusion: A Service, Not A Place.* (Video and book) Port Chester, NY: National Professional Resources, Inc., 2001.

McGregor, Gail R. Tumm Vogelsburg. *Inclusive Schooling Practices: Pedagogical and Research Foundations.* Baltimore, MD: Paul H. Brookes Publishing, 1998.

National Professional Resources, Inc. (Publisher*). Inclusion Times for Children and Youth With Disabilities* (Newsletter). Port Chester, NY, 2001.

Porter, Stephanie, et al. *Children and Youth – Assisted Medical Technology in Educational Settings: Guidelines for Care*. Baltimore, MD: Paul H. Brookes Publishing, 1997.

Renzulli, Joseph S. *Developing the Gifts and Talents of ALL Students: The Schoolwide Enrichment Model* (Video), Port Chester, NY: National Professional Resources, Inc., 1999.

Rief, Sandra F. *How To Reach and Teach ADD/ADHD Children*. West Nyack, NY: Center for Applied Research in Education, 1993.

Rief, Sandra F. *Inclusive Instruction & Collaboration Practices* (Video), Port Chester, NY: National Professional Resources, Inc., 1995.

Rief, Sandra F. *How To Help Your Child Succeed in School: Strategies and Guidance for Parents of Children with ADHD and/or Learning Disabilities* (Video), Port Chester, NY: National Professional Resources, Inc., 1997.

Scully, Jennifer L. *The Power of Social Skills in Character Development: Helping Diverse Learners Succeed*. Port Chester, NY: National Professional Resources, Inc., 2000.

Sterling, Diane, et al. *Character Education Connections for School, Home & Community: A Guide for Integrating Character Education*. Port Chester, NY: National Professional Resources, Inc. 2000.

Strichart, Stephen S., Charles T. Mangrum II, & Patricia Iannuzzi. *Teaching Study Skills and Strategies to Students with Learning Disabilities, Attention Deficit Disorders, or Special Needs*, 2nd Edition. Boston, MA: Allyn & Bacon, 1998.

Teele, Sue. *Rainbows of Intelligence: Exploring How Students Learn*. Redlands, CA: Sue Teele, 1999.

Teele, Sue. *Rainbows of Intelligence: Raising Student Performance Through Multiple Intelligences* (Video), Port Chester, NY: National Professional Resources, Inc., 2000.

Thurlow, Martha L., Judy L. Elliott, & James E. Ysseldyke. *Testing Students With Disabilities*. Thousand Oaks, CA: Corwin Press, 1998.

Villa, Richard A., & Jacqueline S. Thousand. *Restructuring for Caring and Effective Education*. Baltimore, MD: Paul H. Brookes Publishing, 2000.

Winebrenner, Susan. *Teaching Kids with Learning Difficulties in the Regular Classroom*. Minneapolis, MN: Free Spirit Publishing, 1998.

Yeager, John, et al. *Character and Coaching: Building Virtue in Athletic Programs*. Port Chester, NY: National Professional Resources, Inc. 2001.